Over 100 Years of Faith in God

The Story of Sister Tonsa Warner

(1902-2005)

By

Nancy A. Link, Ph.D.

author HOUSE®

AuthorHouse™ LLC
1663 Liberty Drive
Bloomington, IN 47403
www.authorhouse.com
Phone: 1-800-839-8640

Published by AuthorHouse   10/03/2013

ISBN: 978-1-4208-1221-3 (sc)

This book is printed on acid-free paper.

Over 100 Years of Faith in God
The Story of Sister Tonsa Warner

**"Now faith is the substance of things hoped for,
the evidence of things not seen" (Hebrews 11:1, KJV).**

Tonsa Nella Fuqua Lavett Warner at about 39 Years of Age

Over 100 Years of Faith in God
The Story of Sister Tonsa Warner

One Woman's Story of Faith

"Honor thy father and thy mother that thy days may be long upon the land which the Lord thy God giveth thee"
(Exodus 20:12, KJV).

This book is dedicated to my Savior, Creator, and Best Friend, The Lord God Almighty, and to the late Sister Tonsa Warner, a great woman of faith who spent her life in humble service to God and others and demonstrated how faith in God works every time.

Table of Contents

Foreword xiii

Chronological Overview of Events..xvii

CHAPTER ONE: Baptized in a Pond 1

CHAPTER TWO: My Family of Eleven....................................7

CHAPTER THREE: West Virginia to Virginia 19

CHAPTER FOUR: The Early 1900's in Washington, DC 29

CHAPTER FIVE: An Exquisite Exhibit of Pictorial Memoirs 37

CHAPTER SIX: Almost 20 Years Later and Beyond 51

CHAPTER SEVEN: Forsaking All I Trust Him 63

CHAPTER EIGHT: Healthy & Happy At 101 Years of Age 72

CHAPTER NINE: Great is God's Faithfulness 81

CHAPTER TEN: Words of Wisdom for Today's Times.......................90

CHAPTER ELEVEN: Quotations and Poetic Salutations..................104

In Summary 115

Foreword

The purpose of this story was to elicit Sister Tonsa Warner's story about how faith in God has been connected to her decision making throughout her life of over 100 years. Metaphorical and technical styles of writing have been utilized to introduce to some and present to others the many facets of Tonsa Nella Fuqua Lavett Warner's journey of faith.

Oh, what a remarkable story of one woman's determination to utilize her gift of faith in God to make it through moment by moment! It was an honor and a privilege to be able to interview Sister Tonsa Warner and share her story in written form with you, dear readers. Since I have viewed writing as exciting for as long as I can remember, I now will shift gears and metaphorically explain my rationale for this story with poetic lines of faith.

Poetic Lines of Faith

To talk with my friend about days gone by,
Days of laughter and days she had to cry.
Storytelling was the tool my friend used to share,
Memories of yesteryear mingled with lots of prayer.

I was driving down Pennsylvania Ave. in DC one day,
When I felt a strong impression to write this story okay?
I wasn't sure about the task, but I asked anyway,
Without hesitation, Sister Warner said, "Yes, okay."

So, as you read about Tonsa Warner's life of devotion,
Enjoy the poetic lines of faith & stories with varied emotion.
For I have done my best to deliver Sister Warner's story,
And with all due honor & respect, to God be all the glory!

Submitted to you, dear reader, in the spirit of agape love,
Nancy A. Link, PhD

Who is Tonsa Warner? To Saundra Barnhart (one of her seven grandchildren), she is "Gramp." Saundra has scripted sentiments of her grandmother in a poem she calls, "Along The Way." Saundra's sentimental expressions poetically and preciously portray some terrific times they have had along the way.

ALONG THE WAY
(Gramp)

Thank you for sharing your
time with me of
years ago,
when I was a child of
six or so.

I followed you around in
your garden of love,
flowers and vegetables
blessings from One
that shines above.

I walked with you along
a narrow path,
of berries, honeysuckle,
and the sweet smell
of grass.

We met a couple at the
top of a hill,
kind words of greetings
I still feel.

I will always remember this
special day,
when you and I walked
hand-in-hand along the way.

Saundra Barnhart
Copyright ©August 23, 2003

As the research unfolded, I found it necessary to mention to you, dear readers, the history of the name Lavett. Tonsa's first husband's name was Harlow Spencer Lovett. However, Harlow and Tonsa's son, McClain Larcello (known affectionately as Bunny), made the critical decision to legally change his last name from Lovett to Lavett many years ago. In addition, Tonsa Nella Fuqua Lavett Warner, the subject of this story of faith, chose (as her preference) to also adopt the name of Lavett. Therefore, you will notice Mr. Harlow Lovett's name is written in the original family spelling when he is being referenced to in this story. All other references are written as Lavett, thereby making the surnames, Lovett and Lavett, interchangeable throughout this document. Enjoy the reading!

I am forever grateful to God, the Great I Am, for helping me complete Sister Warner's story of faith. To God Almighty be all the glory and power and majesty for His never-ending faithfulness to me!

Chronological Overview of Events

1902 – Tonsa Fuqua was born in Talcott, West Virginia, to Nellie Ann Otey Fuqua and Henry June Fuqua.

1906 – Tonsa moves to Trevillians, Virginia, at an early age.

1910 – As a member of the Baptist church, Tonsa was baptized in a pond.

1910 – Tonsa began sewing clothes and made an apron for her mother. She still designs and makes her own clothes today (2003).

1912 – Tonsa saw her first car (Model T Ford) while walking to the store with her mother. She also recalls their two ox carts they had on their farm in Virginia.

1916 – Tonsa visited Washington, DC, for one month, and worked awhile with her cousin, Charles Porter (and his wife, Stella Porter).

1918 – At the age of sixteen, Tonsa moved to Washington, DC.

1921 – At the age of nineteen, Tonsa married Harlow Lovett.

1922 (August) – Harlow and Tonsa were living in Virginia, and their son, McClain Larcello Lovett, is born in Trevillians, Virginia.

1924 (January) – Harlow and Tonsa Lovett continued to reside in Virginia, and their daughter, Violet Lovett, is born in Trevillians, Virginia.

1924 (February) – Mr. Harlow Lovett returned to Washington, DC, to work and find a home for his family and himself.

1924 (May) – While in Virginia, Tonsa received a telegram that said her husband, Mr. Harlow Lovett, had died of a sudden heart attack.

1924–1940's – Tonsa worked for wealthy White Americans in Washington, DC, to support herself and her family (her 2 small children).

1939 – Tonsa was baptized as a Seventh-day Adventist (SDA) at Ephesus SDA Church in Washington, DC, now Dupont Park SDA Church.

1943 – Tonsa was remarried to Elder Howard David Warner, a Seventh-day Adventist minister.

1949 – Tonsa becomes a vegetarian.

1940's to 1960's – Elder and Sister Warner traveled 48 out of 50 states in America as humble servants of God.

1930's to 1960's – Sister Tonsa Warner designed and made many different kinds of hats.

1969 (July) – Elder H. D. Warner, Sister Warner's husband, dies in the pulpit as he stands to deliver his sermon during the 11:00 service on Sabbath morning.

1970 (February) – After the death of her husband, Sister Warner sells her house in New York and moves back to Washington, DC, to live with her son and his wife.

1970 to 2005 – Sister Tonsa Warner resides in Washington, DC, with her two adult children, McClain Larcello Lavett & Violet Barnhart.

CHAPTER ONE

"Even a child is known by his doings, whether his (or her) work be pure, and whether it be right" (Proverbs 20:11, KJV).

Baptized in a Pond

The days of yesteryear are days not long gone. As a matter of fact, those days continue. Keep reading, and you'll see what I mean. She was born over one hundred years ago in Talcott, West Virginia, and her smile still brightly shines in Y2K3. A woman of high Christian standards, one who doesn't quiver at calling sin by its right name, a centurion who wears the name eloquently and rightly so, a lifetime member of God's army, a faithful soldier of the cross – that's Sister Tonsa Nella Fuqua (Fü kwô) Lavett Warner. Born on April 20, 1902, to Henry June and Nellie Ann Fuqua, Sister Tonsa Warner remembers her early years and moving from Talcott, West Virginia, to Trevillians, Virginia, at the age of three (almost four). Growing up on a Virginia farm was so much fun as she recalled the hearty times she spent with her father and mother, and eight brothers and sisters.

To get it straight from Tonsa, she tells the story like this, "Well, we were down there in the country, just our family. It was 9 of us, and we just had a good life together. My mother was right there with us all the time. Trevillians, Virginia, (which is between Charlottesville and Richmond) was where we grew up. So, we just made our own life (fun) and enjoyed one another in the family, and we went to church, and to other little things that went on in the country, we'd go to. My mother would let us go, and we enjoyed our family."

Tonsa went on to say, "We grew up in the Baptist Church, and I was baptized in there when I was a youngster (laughing), baptized in a pond. This was a pond where the trains had come in and they'd pump the water from the pond to fill the train. They had to put so much water in there. I don't know. They had 'coal trains.' They were run by coal, not by electricity like so many of them are run today. So, I was baptized in the pond at 7 or 8 years old."

She spoke fondly of her four brothers and four sisters. She remembered her oldest sister living to be about 93. According to Tonsa, she (her oldest sister, Lucinda June) lived in Richmond, Virginia, and when she was in her 80's, Tonsa and Taqua (Tonsa's youngest sister) went to Richmond and helped Lucinda move to Washington, DC, where she resided at the Mayfair Apartments complex. Then Lucinda got sick, and they had to put her in a nursing home. At the time, as Tonsa stated, "I had had an operation on my back, and I couldn't do for her, and my other sister (Taqua) was working full time. So Lucinda went in the nursing home, and she didn't stay there too long before she passed."

Tonsa's oldest brother, Rossie Otey Fuqua, left home when he was about 18 years old. He went out to work in West Virginia, and he worked for the C&O Railroad for 54 years. Then he retired from there. Another one of her brothers, Richard Stepheny Fuqua, worked in the city of Washington, DC, on different jobs, and he passed away in the 1980's. Tonsa's little brother, McClain, was remembered as a wonderful and adorable child, who passed when he was 6 years old with no apparent cause of death.

All of Tonsa's siblings have passed away except her little sister, Taqua, whom she still affectionately refers to as her 'baby doll.' Taqua presently resides in Washington, DC, and drives everywhere, enjoys spending time outdoors, and they (Tonsa and Taqua) go where they want to go. During the Summer of 2002, Tonsa and her sister, Taqua, took a train ride from Washington, DC, to New Mexico to see a friend, who Sister Warner refers to as being just like another sister. As you read on, you will notice that Chapter 2 expounds more on Tonsa's 8 brothers and sisters.

Oh What Fun
By Nancy A. Link, Ph.D.

Oh what fun they always had,
Serving God made them glad.
Good times were always there,
She knew God really did care.

During the interviews with Sister Tonsa Warner, I asked many questions, and she gave rich and wonderful answers. Sometimes, unexpected events surfaced. Yet, that's to be expected, right? In our first interview, I asked Sister Warner to tell me what faith meant to her, and her reply was as follows. "Faith means everything, everything, yes. If you can't work a thing out, just leave it in His hands. Don't worry about it. Say, Lord, You take this. It's too hard for me. Yes, You can work it out. I can't."

As Sister Warner reminisced about her early days in Trevillians, Virginia, she recalled her family always being Christians and growing up in the Baptist Church. Being an obedient child was something that was always important to her, especially being obedient to her parents and to God. Living out in the country in Trevillians, Virginia, a town between Charlottesville and Richmond, Tonsa recalls the joy of being baptized in a pond around the age of eight. Laughter, excitement, spiritual fulfillment, and more was expressed as she shared these moments of yesteryear.

Reflections of Faith
By Nancy A. Link, Ph.D.

I am over 100 now, but I was about 8 *then*,
Praise God, I still know Him as *Friend*.
It was a blessing to my soul in *1910*,
I tell you my child, I would do it *again*.
Nothing but dirt roads back in the *day*,
We loved God & each other *anyway*.
Baptized in a pond seems long *gone*,
Praise God, though, for Jesus, His *son*.

Tonsa Fuqua Lavett at about 30 Years of Age

In the words of Sister Tonsa Fuqua Lavett Warner, "Everyday is a good day. God has blessed me. I'm able to live 'cause you not gonna carry anything with you anyway. As long as you live, as long as you have a few clothes to put on, food to eat, and a place to live with a roof over your head, that's all you need. And that's what I thank God for every morning – the life He has given to me and for watching over me. I've made mistakes just like everybody else, but God is there. You make one, you don't go and make another one."

Sister Warner's prayer each morning is, "Lord give me strength for this day, and guide me in the right way, and let me help anybody I can help in any way possible." I just pray all the time. I don't know any special time to pray. I just pray all the time, all during the day, just stop and pray. When I get in the car, I ask God to carry us and bring us back. Everything I do, I have faith to believe that it's His Will, not mine, 'cause you know, sometimes we want things that's not going to benefit us, but if it's God's will, He'll give it in His way – maybe not the way I ask for it or want it, but it's His will.

Tonsa Fuqua Lavett at about the age of 25

From being baptized as an eight-year old child to facing life as a centurion, one might look back and say, God has mightily blessed Sister Warner. He has allowed her to look back down 'Memory Lane' and see that He's brought her through and continues to bless her everyday. For as she would say in the words of her favorite song, "God did it all *just for me*." In the next chapter, Sister Warner, gifted with total recall, allows us to reminisce with her as she remembers her family of eleven.

****

CHAPTER TWO

****

**"Even a child is known by his doings, whether his (or her) work
be pure, and whether it be right"
(Proverbs 20:11, KJV).**

My Family of Eleven

Family times bring back the best of times and sometimes, the not so best of times, and God was and is always there for Sister Tonsa Warner. In her narrative voice, she articulated, "My mother instilled in the children some good values, which sticks with me today," over one hundred one years after she was born in the United States of America in the state of West Virginia. As Sister Warner's mother, Nellie Ann Otey Fuqua, always said to her children, "Do what's right and you'll always make it." These simple words of advice are remembered by Tonsa as she continues her journey of faith as a centurion.

As Tonsa recalls, her parents were hard working, loving, kind, and devoted, and they always expressed good family values. Henry June Fuqua, born on March 15 c1868, in Bedford, Virginia, and Nellie Ann Otey Fuqua, born on August 10, c1875, on the edges of the Emancipation Proclamation, instilled in their nine children "*faith in God through it all.*"

When asked what the main thing was she remembered about her father, Tonsa replied, "He was a hard working man who took care of his family." Although she was very young, 3 or 4 years old, Tonsa remembered and mentioned that her dad also worked in the coal mines of West Virginia. Nellie Ann and Henry June Fuqua trained their children in the way they should go, and Tonsa Nella continues to demonstrate obedience to right living. Even today, as a senior of over 100 years, she won't depart from her parents' training.

Besides Tonsa Nella, Henry June and Nellie Ann had eight other wonderful children back during the late 1890's and early 1900's. Joy was expressed in Sister Warner's voice as she reminisced about her siblings. The names of Henry June and Nellie Ann Fuqua's children follow: Lucinda June Fuqua Gravett (1895); Rossie Otey Fuqua (1898); Emma Ophelia Fuqua Tolson(1900); Tonsa Nella Fuqua Lavett Warner (1902); Henry Jester McClain Fuqua (1903); McClain Fuqua (1905); Richard Fuqua (1906); Calestard Elizabeth Fuqua (1912); and Taqua Ollie Fuqua Trescott (1914).

All of Sister Warner's brothers and sisters have slipped away to death except Taqua Ollie Fuqua Trescott, and oh what fun Tonsa continues to have with her little sister, Taqua. Let's reflect on the summer of 2002 when Tonsa and Taqua took a train ride from Washington, DC, to the state of New Mexico to visit their friend, who had recently gotten married at 87 years old, or should I say, "87 years young?"

Oh, I would have loved to have gone on that cross country journey with Tonsa and Taqua, but like you, I got the story second hand, but that's okay. According to Sister Warner, the trip was wonderful. It took her and her sister about two (2) days to travel cross country on the train and the same amount of time to travel back to Washington, DC. Sister Warner has flown via plane before but stated, "I have never ridden an airplane to New Mexico, and I don't want to either." They visited with their friend for two weeks, and Sister Warner stated that they simply enjoyed themselves.

After returning from New Mexico, Sister Warner was hospitalized because as she stated, "I was just tired. I didn't feel well. So, my children took me to the hospital." After some resting and testing, Sister Warner shared with me that the doctors and nurses were very surprised at her excellent state of health for a woman of her age. However, she gives God all the praise, honor, and glory. She knows that it's God and God alone who keeps her strong.

Born the 4th of nine (9) children, Tonsa Nella Fuqua Lavett Warner excitedly expressed the closeness and love that was always the glue that held their family together. In the words that follow, Sister Warner reminisced about her parents and brothers and sisters, her family of eleven, whom she has loved from the start and continues to love dearly.

Lucinda June Fuqua, born June 1, 1895, was the oldest girl. Tonsa's words, "We worked on the farm together and listened to Mother. We had horses, cows, and chickens, and everything we needed to eat. Mother canned everything we ate. My mother, my sister Lucinda, and the rest of us made bread, hot bread, loaf bread, and it lasted through the week. We had hogs for the winter, and we just had plenty to eat. We carried eggs and butter to the store and traded our goods for what we needed, like coffee or sugar. There were no deep freezers like people have today. We dug a trench and buried our food and covered it with leaves and dirt. This would keep the food cool and fresh all winter, foods like potatoes and apples. It was our way of refrigerating it."

When asked what she mostly remembered about her sister, Lucinda, Sister Warner said she didn't remember a lot. She stated that her oldest sister, seven (7) years older than she was, left home at 16 to go to Philadelphia, Pennsylvania, to work, and she would come home about every five (5) years to see the family. Lucinda married Mr. Leonard Gravett, and they had two (2) sons, Leonard Jr. and Rossie.

Because of strong family ties, Leonard and Lucinda Gravett's two (2) sons came to stay with Lucinda's parents and siblings around 1914 while their parents stayed in Philadelphia to work. Tonsa remembers Leonard Jr. and Rossie very well because they were young children when they moved in with them, and as Tonsa recollected, "They grew up with us." After many years of living in Pennsylvania, Lucinda returned to Virginia (Richmond).

Tonsa's sister, Lucinda, eventually moved to Washington, DC, when she was about 80 years old. She lived in her own apartment, and Tonsa and her youngest sister, Taqua, took care of her. Sister Warner stated, "Lucinda was kind of crippled in her legs and was taken to the hospital one day because she was not feeling well. Later, she went to a nursing home and passed away at the age of 93."

On May 23, 1898, Tonsa's eldest brother, Rossie Otey Fuqua, was born. In his sister's own words, "Rossie Otey was a very responsible person and looked after the family because Father was a coal miner."

According to Tonsa, their father would be gone for months at a time, and Rossie was that watchful eye around the house. As Tonsa said, "Our mother did the directing of the children, but Brother Rossie acted like he was our father and looked out for us." She also recalled Rossie Otey going to work on the railroad in Montgomery, West Virginia, for 54 years before he retired.

Tonsa's brother, Rossie, married Beatrice Morris, and she passed away about one (1) year after they were married. Tonsa said Beatrice just got sick and passed on. In Tonsa's narrative voice, "Rossie's second wife was Susie Fuqua, and they had two (2) children, Ann and Rossie. Everybody supported everybody. Rossie, Susie, and their two (2) children lived and worked in West Virginia. Having lived a good life, Rossie passed away at 84 from old age. We went to West Virginia to bury him."

On July 8, 1900, Tonsa's second oldest sister, Emma Ophelia Fuqua, who was affectionately called "Pete," was born. In Tonsa's words, "We grew up together. She was my buddy." We all played together, sewed, and made baby doll clothes together for our little sisters." According to Tonsa, they called their little sisters, Calestard and Taqua, "baby dolls." She further articulated, "Pete and I cooked pies and cakes, and sometimes they didn't come out too good, but they were good to us, and we had lots of fun on our farm doing things together."

Tonsa joyfully recalled the first thing she made (sewed). She was 8 years old, and she made an apron for her mother. Now, her sister and buddy, Pete, was right there encouraging her as she stitched her first garment. Her brother, Henry Jester, also gave her a hand in sewing the apron for their mother. Now, at 101 years old, Sister Tonsa Fuqua Lavett Warner still makes her own clothing and does a superb job at it too.

When asked about what Emma Ophelia "Pete" did when she left home, Tonsa simply stated, "Wasn't nothing to do but work for the White folks – cleaning, cooking, washing, ironing, or any other housework you could do." She further stated, "Colored men chauffeured if they got jobs like that, but the Colored girls would get jobs sweeping floors and were categorized as *dining room girls, upstairs girls, cooking girls, or laundry girls.* Yes, a colored girl might have her own quarters if she worked for the White folks." Tonsa spoke about how they worked in the fields for themselves (because they had their own farm) but not for anyone else "like the Colored people who were farther South."

Emma Ophelia left Virginia and came to Washington, DC, at about the age of 16. In her 20's, she married Frank Tolson, and they had one (1) son, Charles Tolson. She did domestic work, and her husband was a driver for the White folks. In a very straightforward way, Sister Warner spoke clearly, "Nobody Colored sat behind a desk working in government, teaching, or in the stores. If you went in a store and tried something on or bought it and it didn't fit, it was yours. Colored people had to ride on the back of streetcars too." Then, Sister Warner commented on today's times, "Young Colored people don't understand or appreciate what the older people went through for them."

Tonsa declared that her sister, Pete, "smoked too much." Tonsa asked Pete the question one day, "Why don't you give up that smoking?" Pete's reply was, "Ah, you got to die from something." Although Tonsa has never in her life drank alcohol or smoked, she strongly believes Pete's urge to smoke started when she (Pete) used to light their grandmother's pipes. In Tonsa's words, "That's what I think got her (my sister Pete) started. Grandmother was a slave early in her life, and maybe," Tonsa speculated, "that's what drove my grandmother to smoking." Emma

Ophelia "Pete" was 62 when she died, and Tonsa simply declared, "She smoked too much!"

Tonsa Nella Fuqua Lavett Warner remembers her siblings very well and reminisces of the days of yesteryear just as if it was yesterday. Her second oldest brother's name was Henry Jester McClain Fuqua, who was born on Christmas 1903. As Tonsa stated, "He was next to me in age." She remembers Henry Jester as being a nice young man. They played together and had good times at home since there was no entertainment like movies, television, or radio.

In the words of Henry Jester's sister, Tonsa, "We just all grew up together and had a good time together working on the farm. We all did our work. The girls did the cooking, cleaning, and sewing. The boys did their chores of bringing in the wood for the stove in the kitchen and took care of the livestock." They had no oil lamps, electric lights, telephones, or anything like the modern technology we enjoy today.

Tonsa talked about how Henry Jester and the rest of the children would play the victrola (record player). She talked about how they had records that their father would bring home to them when he would come in from his strenuous mining jobs. According to Tonsa's recollection, "We could only listen to church music." She mentioned that there were different kinds of music, but their mother was a faithful Christian and would only allow them to listen to inspirational music. Then, I asked if they danced to the music, and Sister Warner giggled and sternly replied, "You didn't dance in my mother's house."

In remembering Henry Jester, Tonsa happily spoke about how all of her brothers and sisters played together and went to school together, which stopped at 4th grade for most of the Colored children. It was interesting to find out from Sister Tonsa Warner her perspective of the teachers back during her school days. She declared, "The teachers didn't know much. My mother would help us at home. She would help us work the arithmetic problems out and send the work back to school with us. My mother had a great mind. She could work anything out. She knew more than the teachers."

Now back to Henry Jester! He decided to relocate to Washington, DC, around the year 1917 to make a living. He was married to Rosa Douglass, who was a housewife. Henry Jester's first job was in Alexandria, Virginia, working outside in White people's yards doing landscaping and working around homes. He was then able to find a good job in Washington, DC, driving for the grocery stores. Henry Jester worked really hard and did a good job taking care of his wife and himself. Although they never had any children, everybody in Tonsa's family had been taught to go to church. She stated that they all continued going to church over the years, even her brother Henry Jester and his wife, Rosa.

At the age of about 25, Tonsa's brother, Henry Jester, was in a car accident, and after being hit by another car, which caused his car to turn over, he never recuperated. He lived for several days, but then he succumbed to fatal injuries from the accident.

Henry and Nellie Fuqua's 6th child and 3rd son, born in July 1905, was McClain Fuqua. After living a very short life with a wonderfullyloving family, McClain passed away quietly at the age of 6, nobody really knowing the cause of his death. As Sister Warner recalled, "He just got sick and passed on."

On December 28, 1907, Tonsa's 4th brother, Richard Fuqua, was born. She remembers Richard as being a typical child, growing up with all of them, playing together and working in the fields and gardens. Just like Henry Jester, Richard played with his siblings and did the things that the boys were to do around the house and on their farm. As stated previously, the boys did their chores of bringing in the wood for the stove in the kitchen and took care of the livestock. The children all grew up together and had a good time together working on the farm under the direction of their mother while their father worked in the coal mines.

Again, another daughter was born to the Fuqua family. Her name was Calestard Elizabeth Fuqua, and she was born in September 1912. As Tonsa traveled down 'Memory Lane', she admitted that she looked at and treated Calestard Elizabeth like a baby doll. Delightfully, Tonsa voiced, "She (Calestard) was such a cute baby, and we just played with her. We made her clothes, which we called baby doll clothes, and she was just so much fun to play with." After Calestard Elizabeth grew up, she also moved to Washington, DC, to be close to the rest of her siblings, for the exception of Rossie Otey, who continued to reside in Montgomery, West Virginia.

As told by Sister Tonsa Warner, Calestard Elizabeth came to Washington, DC, to work. Although she was never married, she secured a job doing housework, and this is what she did during her lifetime to make a living. Sister Warner continues to be reminiscent of their wonderful days together as she articulated, "Calestard Elizabeth passed away in June 1946, and there was no cause of death. She just took sick and went down, down, down."

On August 21, 1914, Henry and Nellie Fuqua were blessed with their 9th child and 5th daughter, Taqua Ollie Fuqua. Tonsa's sentimentality toward Taqua started from the first moment she saw her as a babe. Just like Calestard Elizabeth, Taqua was loved and adored as a "baby doll." Listen to Tonsa's words, "I just took her as my doll baby. All of us were friends, a loving family, helping one another, doing things for one another. I just took her and dressed her up. When I was working (in Washington, DC), I would remember them and send them something back home in Virginia. If something was going on at church, I'd also send them something nice to wear."

Taqua moved to Washington, DC, in 1932, at the youthful age of 19. Eleven years later, she was married to Mr. Charles Trescott in November 1943. As time went by, Taqua was able to work in the Pentagon and for the Food and Drug Administration behind desks, which many Colored people weren't able to do. She also worked for the Department of Defense (Air Force) and is now retired. Charles Trescott, Taqua's husband, also worked for the federal government for the Federal Reserve. Charles preceded Taqua in death in 1995 and is dearly missed by his family and friends. Taqua is a wonderful person, very kind hearted, and a superb cook. She resides in Washington, DC, and has the gifts of smiling, cooking, driving, and down home hospitality.

Now, let's look at Sister Warner's words as she reflects family values. "Children didn't roam the streets. They came in before dark and respected what the parents said. Otherwise, you would be on the floor if you said the wrong thing. I speak to children now whether they like it or not. Children shouldn't question parents and be disrespectful to adults."

As for marriage and the family, Sister Warner stated, "I had a grand and glorious marriage. It was great getting him (my husband) off to work and having his dinner fixed when he came home at night. My husband thought I was the most perfect wife ever." Tonsa summed her family up by saying, "All of us were friends, a loving family, helping one

Over 100 Years of Faith in God

another, doing things for one another!" In Chapter 3, let's travel from West Virginia to Virginia with Tonsa during her childhood days.

A Horse and Buggy from the days of yesteryear

17

Over 100 Years of Faith in God
by Nancy A. Link, Ph.D.

Over 100 years of faith in God,
Believing for God, nothing's too hard,
After she's done all, Tonsa Warner can stand,
And say, "God is real," throughout the land.

Over 100 years of faith in God,
Knowing God is love & confirming it with a nod.
I thank Tonsa Warner for sharing her story,
And to our great Jehovah belongs all the glory.

Over 100 years of faith in God,
Protecting us is God's shield and rod.
Tonsa Warner's testimony came by many tests,
And no matter what, God will always deliver His best.

Over 100 years of faith in God,
Telling you to keep the faith as 'this land' you trod,
Tonsa Warner is one of God's servants who rejoices,
And I praise God for His people's worshipping voices.

```
*********************************************************************
```

CHAPTER THREE

```
*********************************************************************
```

"Who can find a virtuous woman? For her price is far above rubies" (Proverbs 31:10, KJV).

West Virginia to Virginia

Not so far away and not very long ago, the words of a devoted wife and mother could be heard by her charming children whom she had taught well to trust and obey God through it all. The mother that I have reference to is Mrs. Nellie Ann Otey Fuqua. In Chapter 2, you met her nine children and hard working husband. So, as you can probably tell, Mother Nellie Fuqua was a praying woman who believed in family and togetherness.

As a little girl, Tonsa fondly recalls how her mother trusted the Lord in everything and taught her children to treat everybody right. In Tonsa's words, "Nobody (none of my brothers or sisters) has ever been to jail or anything, and I look forward to meeting my mother in Heaven. We had a beautiful life together as a family. Don't mess with one of us or everybody jumped in. We were always together."

During our second interview, May 27, 2002, Sister Warner referred to the fact that our foreparents had faith in God. She reminded me of how books can be read on how our ancestors would get together at night time, and they would sing and pray when they wanted to do something, and that was how they came out of slavery.

Although Tonsa's mother was never a slave, her grandmother and grandfather (her mother's parents) did experience the cruelty of living as slaves. As a matter of fact, Tonsa's grandparents met on a slave plantation, where they fell in love and were married. Resultantly, it was the Lord in His mercy and grace that brought them all through it all.

Tonsa Nella Fuqua was born in Talcott, West Virginia, on Sunday, April 20, 1902. The president of the United States at that time was Theodore Roosevelt, and there were some very interesting events occurring on that date. The United States Senate voted to extend the Chinese Exclusion Act for the second time, which barred Chinese immigration into America for another 10 years. Also, in the state of Texas, the Texas Company was formed.

According to the research, on April 20, 1902, this new oil company (the Texas Company) had hopes of challenging Standard Oil's humongous monopoly in the oil industry. Furthermore, people continued looting and rioting across Russia because of a terrible famine causing destruction to over 80 estates in that country. To make matters worse, Jim Crow laws made life miserable for many people of color in America (particularly

African Americans). Regardless of the times, the Fuqua family prayed together and stayed together.

Moving from West Virginia to Virginia is vague in Tonsa's memory. She and her family moved to a farmhouse in Louisa County, Virginia, (town of Trevillians) when she was about 4 years old. The only thing she remembered about West Virginia was her father working in the coal mines and wearing a little hat with a light on it like one might see in the movies today. If someone was hurt in the coal mines, one of the miners would blow the whistle. Tonsa still remembers to this day what her mother was saying to her oldest sister, Lucinda, one day, almost 100 years ago, "Run, run, see who's hurt!" This warning cry was made because all the women would go running to see if it was their husband who had gotten hurt. This was the only thing Tonsa remembered about West Virginia because she was just a little child of 3 or 4 years old when they moved to Virginia.

From 4 to 16 years old, Tonsa lived in Louisa County, Virginia. They lived, loved the Lord and one another, laughed, landscaped, and labored on their Virginia farm. Among the exciting and sometimes not so exciting moments, they grew vegetables, and tended cows, chickens, and hogs. Mother Nellie Fuqua was known as a strict disciplinarian and as Tonsa verbalized, "My mother didn't let us run all over the creation." There were 9 children, and as Tonsa stated, they made their own entertainment at home.

As we journey back in time to relive the main events of Tonsa's birth year and early years from West Virginia to Virginia, it is amazing to just think about it all. Back during the early 1900's, there were no electric lights but lamps, and no furnaces but fireplaces and stoves in the homes.

The following graphic depiction, as revealed by Tonsa, displays the cost of living in the early 1900's vs. the early 2000's.

Cost of Living Chart
(from Tonsa Warner's memory files)
©2003 Nancy A. Link, Ph.D.

	Early 1900's	Early 2000's
Average Annual Income	$360.00	$25,000.00
Dozen Eggs	.10	$1.49
Gallon of Milk	.00 (Had cows)	$2.99
Gallon of Gasoline	.06	$1.49
Lamp Oil (1900's) Electric Lights (2000's)	$2.00 (monthly)	$75.00 (monthly)
Loaf of Bread	.05	$1.95
New Car	$400.00	$21,000.00
New House (93 Acres of Farmland)	$350.00	-millions-
Pair of Shoes	$2.50	$75.00
Pound of Country Butter	0.12	$2.49
Teacher's Salary	$264.00	$30,000.00

Tonsa recalls spending a lot of quality time with her mother, Nellie. In Tonsa's words, "Well, my mother was a Christian. She believed in God. We never heard anything about Seventh-day Adventists, but there was something about Saturday. We called it Saturday. We went to church on Sunday, but there was something about Saturday. We didn't do a lot of work on this day. My mother would just prepare for the next day to go to church, like cooking, washing up, and taking our baths, and be ready for Sunday morning to go to church, and that's the way we were brought up. She was a Christian. She believed in God. Saturday was still special. It was something about it (Saturday) compared to the other days, but she didn't know why."

On another memorable note, Tonsa declared, "You know people back then. They didn't talk to children like they talk to them now. You didn't get into grown people's conversations. When the people would come to the house, you would go out and play. The only person I knew in my father's family was one sister and an uncle because he didn't say anything about it. His mother died when he was young, and at that time, different ones would take children and raise them, and then they would lose contact with their family."

Going back to school days, Tonsa also spoke about how she remembered her first teacher. She mentioned that her teacher got $22 a month. In her narrative voice, she verbalized, "That's what our Colored teachers got paid when I was going to school, and you only had 4 months (November, December, January, and February) of schooling every year. Then, at the end of February, you were out of school. They had White Superintendents over schools, no Coloreds, and they didn't care whether you learned or not. They didn't care what went on in the schools."

Tonsa went on to say, "The thing about it, I don't know where my mother got her information and schooling. She could tell you just what to do. She had a good mind, and she believed in things that were right and she put that in us, to do the thing that was right, and you can always make it. She was a good teacher, and she was pretty good at everything. See, the teachers we had weren't really graduates from high school. What they did (the leaders) was just pick somebody out and put them in the schools as teachers."

According to Tonsa's impression of the teachers, "They (the teachers) didn't know much. So my mother would sit down and teach us arithmetic (called Math today). She would keep you in that arithmetic and work it out and help us work it out. Mother would work it out and then send us back to school. She read a lot and understood what she read and had the gift of learning I guess."

In Tonsa's very humble way, she calmly declared, "I never smoked or drank or anything like that – never ever. I never was just out into something – like I didn't know what I was doing. I would think about my mother and what she would be teaching us as children. She said, 'Be a lady,' and that's what I tried to be in helping others." Sister Tonsa Lavett Fuqua Warner's parents were very special to her. Although her mother was not a Seventh-day Adventist, Tonsa remembers her as a strict Christian who taught her children about God, and Sister Nellie Fuqua told them that "God was and should always be first in your life."

As a young child and adolescent in Virginia, Tonsa has recollections of many fun-filled days with her parents and brothers and sisters. As Sister Warner articulated, "With growing up in the country, you didn't have all this stuff the children have today. You made your own fun."

On one occasion, Sister Tonsa Warner reflected on seeing her first car as she walked to the store one day with her mother. She recalled being about 10 or 11 years old and asking her mother about this interesting motorized contraption. Now that she looks back, she remembers that old Ford like it was yesterday. In her words, as she laughed jovially, "The first car I saw was in 1912 or 1913 (in Trevillians, VA) coming through the country. My mother and I were walking to the store one day and this little thing came down the road, and I didn't even know what it was." Laughing, she continued by saying, "It was a car. I have no idea what kind of car that was, probably a Ford, since that was the first one put out."

Looking back to those Virginian days of long ago, Tonsa jovially shares her recollections of the ox cart and horses and buggies. She tells her story as follows. "We had an ox cart at our home in Virginia. Two oxen pulled the wagon, and then we got rid of the oxen and got horses, and they pulled the wagon. Whatever we had to move like wood that we'd cut for fire and other stuff we had to carry, we'd use the ox cart for. Just like cars and trucks today, we used the horses and buggy for back then. We would get dressed up, and we had our buggy to ride to church in, and when we didn't have a horse and buggy, sometimes we went to church in the ox cart. That's the way we went to church."

Later, during the interviews with Sister Warner, she shared more exciting history with me about their days with the ox carts. "Well you used them, the oxen, just like you would horses. You'd hitch them up to the wagon, the plow. You'd haul wood and things like that. We moved to Virginia in 1906, and we had them, the ox carts, for about 4 years or so. We rode in the ox carts. That was our transportation. I never liked animals. I was afraid of them, and my brothers and sisters could ride the horses, but not me. I was afraid of the horses."

Tonsa went on to say, "We had 2 oxen that we hitched to the wagon, one on one side and the other one on the other side, and the thing in the middle. You drove them just like you would a horse. Then we got a mule, and then horses. We just had the horses then. So, before the ox carts, we walked. I don't remember if the ox died or we sold them. We kept the buggies and wagons." Tonsa also reflected on seeing her first car by saying, "I think the first car I saw, I was walking to the store with my mother, and I said, 'Mama, what is that?'" and they just kept on walking.

Yes, as Sister Warner recalled, her family always worked together and loved one another. As she eloquently articulated, "We'd just do things together and get joy, and we thought that was the way of life." Even as a child, including the early teenage years, Tonsa felt like everyday was good to her because God blessed her over and over again.

When I asked her if she ever dated during her early teen years, Sister Warner smiled gracefully and replied, "No I didn't do too much of that growing up because my mother was strict on us, and you didn't get out. Some of the young men would want to come to the house, but they'd better not. But, I left home when I was 16, and I never got into that dating and all of that. I had dates (after I was on my own), but it wasn't what I wanted. It wasn't for me. I never liked a rough person, a person that drank, cussed, or any of that. That wasn't my life. I enjoyed a quiet life. My brother-in-law introduced me to my first husband, Mr. Harlow Lovett, in Washington, DC." Sister Warner caused my mind to reflect to God's Word, particularly the 5th Commandment, which commands, "Honor thy father and thy mother that thy days may be long upon the land which the Lord thy God giveth thee, (Exodus 20:12, KJV)" as she further elaborated, "When I was growing up, I believed what my mother was teaching us, the way of life, the better way of life, and I always tried to keep that in mind. And even when my mother had to go to the store in the winter, she'd fix a fire, and she said, 'I don't want anybody to move now until I get back,' and we'd sit around the fireplace. I just thought it was a great thing for me to sit there until she got back, and my other sisters and brothers, they'd get up and start to playing and carrying on, but I wouldn't move out of that chair. I just felt good for myself that I had done what she told me to do. Yes, I loved being obedient to my parents."

Sister Tonsa Lavett Warner sincerely stressed her viewpoints by saying, "I am able to live, and you're not going to carry nothing with you anyway. As long as you can live, and have a few clothes to put on and food to eat and a place, with shelter over your head, that's all you need. And that's what I thank God for every morning, the life He has given me and for watching over me. I make mistakes just like everybody else, but God is there. You make one. Then, you don't go and make another one." Surely, Sister Warner has a story of a grandiose magnitude to share with us. She has continued to praise God Almighty through it all, and oh what a blessing it is to write about the strength, faith, and endurance of this sensational centurion!

Sister Warner remembered very little about World War I, and stated, "No, I don't remember a lot from World War I because we were living in the country, and there wasn't a whole lot of newspapers and things like that or television." So much has happened in her life, just like the many soldiers who have gone on before her, but isn't it grand to read the story of this graceful and grand great, great, great, great grandmother?

My dear friend, Sister Tonsa Lavett Warner, allows one to get a glimpse of her on-going faith in God when she simply utters, "It's just so many things that you know that God was in it." Furthermore, she adds, "And you just keep on trying to live better because it's too much going on here to give it (your life) to anything here (on earth). You want to make it into that home with Him (God). Then we can all sit together and He

(God) can be our teacher. That's why I pray for my children everyday, 'Lord, just turn them around if they will see the Light before it's too late.'"

Harlow and Tonsa's children, Violet (left) and McClain (right)

Growing up isn't that easy to do, But God will always take care of you.

Take it from Sister Tonsa Warner, God is there around every corner.

As we continue on to the next chapter, Faith in God, the enemy can't capture.

It's the early 1900's in Washington, DC, In Tonsa's words, "God did it just for me."

Tonsa and her first husband, Harlow Lovett

Harlow Lovett, his wife (Tonsa), and their son, McClain (about 2 years old)

```
*************************************
```

CHAPTER FOUR

```
*************************************
```

"God is our refuge and strength, a very present help in trouble"
(Psalm 46:1, KJV).

The Early 1900's in Washington, DC

Traveling down the corridors of the early 1900's in Washington, DC, one comes to appreciate the fond memories and strenuous struggles of that time period in American History, especially when seen from the perspective of Tonsa Nella Fuqua Lavett. Some of the themes that emerge from this story of one woman's life of faith and devotion to God, family, and friends are: love, survival, family, friends, joy, faithfulness, hope, strength, and prayer.

In expounding on Sister Warner's days of yesteryear, her early days in DC during the early 1900's, I now share with you, dear reader, words of hope as quoted from Tonsa's narrative voice. "I grew up in Virginia.

I left Virginia when I was 16 and moved to Washington, DC, to work. I was born in Talcott, West Virginia, and my mother moved to Trevillians, Virginia, in 1906, and we bought a big farm down there. I was born in 1902, and I was about 4 years old when we moved down there, and I stayed there until I was 16, and it was nothing to do down there. You worked on the farm all day. So, my older sister was over here in Washington, and I asked my mother if I could come here to Washington to get a job and help her. So, I came to Washington, DC."

Memories, memories, memories, metaphorical and sometimes mesmerizing, moved Sister Warner to expound on her days of yonder eloquently and excitedly. Remembering her days as a youngster of 16 years old, she shared, "I went to the movies, nothing exciting, just go to the movies and the dance hall. I loved to dance. I danced awhile, and then I gave it up long before I joined the Seventh-day Adventist Church in 1939 because I remembered what my mother said, 'Christians don't dance.'"

Tonsa voiced her opinion on dancing and issues of gender by saying, "Yes, dancing was good exercise, but now we didn't dance like they dance today. We did the '2-Step, Waltz, the Foxtrot, and the Tango.' It was a pleasure, and you went dressed. Girls looked like girls, and men looked like men. You go in there now, you can hardly tell the men from the women. That's right. They (the men) got their hair all fixed up and everything. That's true, and sometimes you're walking along the street, and you think it's a man, and it's a woman."

The storyteller (Tonsa) went on to explain, "Now, that's one thing – I never wore pants (as a child in my mother's presence). I said, 'God made me a woman. I'll wear my dresses because my mother didn't allow us to wear them (pants). We would slip them (our brothers' pants) on sometimes and she (my mother) would catch you with them on and make you take them off. We were children. You know how they do, just having fun. And she'd catch you with them on, and they'd come off of you (laughing)." As time went on, though, Tonsa learned to appreciate wearing a nice pair of women's slacks every now and then.

Tonsa elaborated further by stating, "I loved the movies and dancing because there was nothing else to do. There was not a whole lot to do in this city (Washington, DC) at that time (1918). They had several music places, and it cost money, and I didn't have the money to go in there. There was an amusement park on Nannie Helen Burroughs Avenue called 'Suburban Gardens.' If you've ever been up Division Avenue, that's where it was. First, it was a cemetery. They moved the bodies out, and then, they built this amusement park up there."

After working in DC for about 3 years, Tonsa shared, "I met my first husband, Harlow, and got married and went home, and my son was born. See, after I got married and got pregnant, I said, 'I don't know anything about raising children.' So, I came home to have the baby 'cause having a baby was a big thing,' I thought. So, I said, 'I'm going home to mama and have my baby.'"

After Harlow and Tonsa were married in Washington, DC, in 1921, they decided to move to Virginia with Tonsa's family for awhile. In Tonsa's words, "So, I stayed there, and then my husband, he came down and stayed there a year and worked with my father. Then, he came back to get an apartment and everything so he could bring me back and the children because both of them had been born and were babies. So, I had just got this letter from him saying, 'I'm getting the apartment, and we'll be together soon.' Two hours after that, I got a telegram saying he had died of a heart attack."

As Tonsa recollected times gone by, she stated, "That's when my children were born, in the 1920's. I got married July 19, 1921, when I was 19. My son was born the next year on August 24, 1922. Then, my daughter was born in 1924 on January 18th, and my husband died in 1924 on May 13th when my daughter wasn't even 4 months old."

Tonsa continued her story by saying, "I was 21, and then I came to Washington, DC, and brought the children with me. They didn't have any day nurseries, and I don't like them anyway. Some of them are good, but I don't like nurseries. So, my mother said, 'Let the children come back home.' So, she came and got them, and that's the way it went. She raised them until they were in their teens, and then they came here and went to school." My response to this brave, Christian woman's story of love, strength, honor, and family was, "That's what family is all about." Quietly, she replied, "That's true, every one helping one another."

The early 1900's in Washington, DC, was more than a notion for Tonsa. As a widow at 21 and a single parent, she knew that God was always there for her to see her through. To support her two young children and herself, she was blessed with what she referred to as a "good job." God has continued to bless Tonsa Fuqua Lavett Warner all her days, and she replied, "He has. He has, and I just look back sometimes and say, 'Why me?'" She went on to say, "And the people I worked for always trusted me. I did the buying for the house, and they never questioned me or what I spent or anything. Whatever I spent, that was it!"

On one occasion, when Tonsa was traveling back to Washington from visiting her children and family in Virginia, she used her narrative voice to take me down 'Memory Lane' once again. "I had gone down to visit my children after my husband died, and this couple was on the bus, and he (the husband) was just coughing, coughing, coughing. It was him, his wife, and 2 little children. Then I said, 'You don't feel well, do you?' He replied, 'No, I don't.' They didn't have but 2 cents in their pockets, and they were trying to get to a hospital in Maryland."

Sister Warner continued, "So when they got to Fredericksburg, Virginia, I said, 'Come on. Let's have dinner.' And he said, 'No, I don't want anything, but if you could feed my children?' because they didn't have any money. So, when I got to the bus station, I tried to get a place for them to stay overnight because he wasn't really able to continue on. So, I went to the bus station, and they said, 'We don't have a place like that.' So at Union Station (Fredericksburg, Virginia), there was a place called the Salvation Army. You could go there and get help."

With the need to help this family heavily on her heart, Sister Warner replied to the individual at Union Station, "He can't even get across the street. So, this White man walked up and said, 'I'll take you.' He said, 'I drive a cab. I'll take you free.' And another White man walked up and gave me $2.00. $2.00 then was like $5.00 now."

After receiving the gracious gift of $2.00 from a passerby, Tonsa went on to say, "So I went to Union Station to the Salvation Army. They said, 'Does he have references or something?' I said, 'Ma'am, the man has served his country. Take him. He's dying. Just give him a place to rest, he and his family tonight. That's what I'm asking for.' And she called the Salvation Army, and they came and got them. And I often wondered what happened to them. They only had 2 cents in their pockets, and I often wondered what happened to them. That was back in the 1930's."

Sister Warner remembered very little about the Great Depression of the 1930's, and she said it didn't hit them too hard. In addition, her second oldest brother, Henry Jester, had a hard time getting work for a little while. Finally, he got somewhat discouraged, but then he went to work, and he was happy.

A simple synopsis of her time spent in Washington, DC, in the early 1900's follows in Sister Warner's words. "There were mostly dirt roads. Horses and buggies were used by a lot of people in the city. Milk wagons were there bringing you milk in the morning, and bread wagons were there bringing you bread and leaving it at your door. We had an amusement park called 'Suburban Gardens,' and my favorite ride was the Caterpillar, which was like a tunnel, and you'd be covered up riding in it." In addition to the sometimes amusing days, Tonsa continued working for wealthy White folks to help her provide for herself and her children.

Tonsa explained her faithful perspective of the ups and downs in her life in Washington, DC, during the early 1900's by declaring, "Well I can say, He (God) has taken care of me. I have never had big jobs because the time I went to work, no Colored girl was sitting behind anybody's desk in this city, no indeed. And the best jobs you had – that you could get – were working for a wealthy family where you'd get your room and board. You didn't have to pay, and with two (2) children, that's what I did, and I worked with good families. I would run the house and everything. I had a car to drive, and I'd run errands and do all the shopping and everything. It was their car (the White family's), but I used it. Whenever I wanted to use it, I'd use it. Faith in God just guided me."

The next chapter delves into an exquisite exhibit of pictorial memoirs. Is a picture really worth a thousand words? Well, Sister Tonsa Lavett Warner is now using the technique of storytelling through photographic memorabilia. What a marvelous display of her story in pictures! What do you say?

The Early 1900's in Washington, DC
By Nancy A. Link, Ph.D.

The early 1900's in Washington, DC,
Saw changes galore, for you and me.
Tonsa Fuqua and many, many others
Made history dear sisters & brothers.

It was 1918 and on into the roaring 20's,
You'd buy some bread for a few pennies.
Radios, movies, and dancing was then in,
Yet, God was always Tonsa's best friend.

Tonsa Fuqua Lavett (Right) and her friend, Lucille Plane (Left), at
World Fair (New York) in 1939

****

CHAPTER FIVE

****

"A word fitly spoken is like apples of gold in pictures of silver"
(Proverbs 25:11, KJV).

An Exquisite Exhibit of Pictorial Memoirs

Harlow Lovett (Tonsa's first husband)

Tonsa (Center), Harlow & Tonsa's son, McClain "Bunny" (Left), and their daughter, Violet "Sis" (Right)

Tonsa Fuqua Lavett standing tall and looking good during the roaring 20's

Tonsa (driver's seat) and her little sister, Calestard (relaxing in back seat), 1924

Tonsa's Parents
Mr. Henry June Fuqua & his wife, Mrs. Nellie Ann Otey Fuqua

Tonsa during the 1920's and 1930's
(Styling, Smiling, and Profiling)

Tonsa's Grandfather, Grandpa Fuqua (Late 1800's)

Tonsa Fuqua at about 17 years of age

Tonsa at about 33 years of age

Tonsa's two young children: McClain (Left) and Violet (Right)

Tonsa's children
McClain "Bunny" at about age 4 and Violet "Sis" at about age 2

Tonsa at about age 26 (Left), her sister, Calestard, at about age 16,
and Tonsa's daughter, Violet "Sis" at about age 5

Bunny (Left) at age 4 and Sis (Right) at age 2

McClain (Bunny) at age 2, Violet (Sis) as an infant, and Charles (Tonsa's nephew) at about age 2

McClain Larcello Lavett "Bunny" at about age 16

Tonsa's mother, Mrs. Nellie Ann Otey Fuqua

McClain Larcello Lovett (Bunny)
at age 5

Tonsa Fuqua Lovett at age 26

Violet Lovett (Sis)
at about age 3

Bunny and Sis enjoying the days of yesteryear, the good times, the great times!
McClain (Bunny) 4 and Violet (Sis) 2

Elder and Sister H. D. Warner
(When they first met)

Tonsa and her little sister, Taqua (Y2K)

As one focuses on the next chapter, which includes words of joy mingled with some tears, Tonsa's story of faith is continued in order to further show how God kept on guiding her throughout her life. It is almost 20 years later and beyond. In other words, you will notice that the next chapter delves into the late 1930's, 1940's, 1950's, 1960's, and beyond. However, let's conclude this chapter with the poem, "Poetic Chapters of our Lives," and a few more pictorial memoirs.

Poetic Chapters of our Lives
Nancy A. Link, Ph.D.

One plus one, poetic chapters of our lives have begun,
Praise God for His people and for His only begotten Son.
There's no need for regret and certainly no need to fret,
For surely, surely, God ain't finished with you or me yet.

Two plus two, poetic chapters of our lives continue,
Praise God for His defense, yes He will defend you.
There are ups and downs and smiles and frowns,
Yet, through it all, God is winner in all the rounds.

Three plus three, poetic chapters of our lives remain,
Praise God for being God and for the joy and the pain.
There are times when it seems like it's time to give up,
But God is real, and He'll help you drink from your cup.

One hundred plus years, poetic chapters with some tears,
Praise God for bringing Tonsa & others through the years.
There may be some words or deeds that have uplifted you,
So, give the best of your service, as only God can help you do.

Tonsa Fuqua Lovett with her 2 small children (McClain and Violet) in 1926 (Top Left); Harlow Lovett (Tonsa's first husband and her children's father) Top Right; and their 2 adult children (Violet and McClain) with their mother, Tonsa, in 2002 (Below)

****

CHAPTER SIX

****

"To every thing there is a season, and a time to every purpose under the heaven" (Ecclesiastes 3:1, KJV).

Almost 20 Years Later and Beyond

Why?

By Nancy A. Link, Ph.D.

Why do we suffer pain?

Why do we cry in the rain?

Why do we go through sorrow?

Why do we hope for tomorrow?

Why do we slowly learn?

Why do we toss and turn?

Why do we sometimes sigh?

Why? God will help us understand it by and by.

Yes, God will help us understand all things better by and by. As I continue traveling down the highways and bi-ways of yesteryear with Sister Tonsa Lavett Warner, I begin to understand better that jubilant joy, joy, unspeakable joy, which is driven by faith in God, as I peer from the outside in. With that said, let's continue traveling with her as she reflects on almost 20 years later and beyond. I am anticipating an overwhelming flood of joy as the pages of Tonsa Nella Fuqua Lavett Warner's history unfold, and maybe you are too, dear reader.

After making it through the decade of the Roaring 1920's, Tonsa faced life with more determination and drive to never ever let go of her faith in God. As a young widow and single parent now, she worked for a wealthy White family in Washington, DC, to help her take care of her children (as was stated earlier in the story). She did the best she knew to do and kindly commented, "Well, where my parents and children lived was about 110 miles from Washington, and you didn't have cars. And when I had the opportunity to spend the night with my children, I would get the bus and go down to Trevillians, Virginia, and visit with them."

In the words of this centurion, "I did this every month or as often as I could because you'd only make a little money. I lived in the house with the White folks. I got my food, and I got my lodging. I didn't have to pay room, rent, or nothing like that. I lived in the home with the family. That's what the Colored girls had to do. You didn't sit in the government behind a desk. I don't care how educated you were. You just didn't get government jobs sitting behind any desk."

Tonsa's story of her early Adventist days was told clearly and memorably also. According to Sister Tonsa Warner's account, it was on March 11, 1939 (a Sabbath), when she was baptized as a Seventh-day Adventist. She shared with me, "I had been going to church and learning about the life of the church, and for about 2 years, I'd been in the church." She then reflected, "So, then, they had a tent effort over here on Nannie Helen Burroughs Avenue here in Washington, DC. The pastor and his wife, who were from the church on 16th Street where I came in, lived right in the back of me, and we met one another, and he (the pastor) said, 'Why don't you come over sometime and join us at the meeting?' So, I went over to the tent meeting, and everybody was so kind and friendly to me. They were so glad to see me and told me to come back again and don't be a perfect stranger."

After a warm reception at the tent meeting, Tonsa remembered saying, "There's something here that I like." Her story continued, "Then, they invited me to go to church with them. I went to church, and then, I began to take Bible studies on Tuesday nights after they asked me if I'd like to go. So, I went to that. I said, "This is what I want." I made up my mind that this is it, and everything would be cut off, the dance hall and everything. That was March 11, 1939, and I was baptized in the Ephesus Seventh-day Adventist Church at 6th and N Streets, NW, Washington, DC."

When Tonsa came to Washington, after her husband, Harlow Lovett, passed away, she was not an Adventist. Then, she decided to be married again about 20 years later. She further tells us, "I was in the church, the Seventh-day Adventist church, and my husband, Elder H. David Warner, was working in Philadelphia at the time, which was 1939."

Quietly listening to Sister Warner on this beautiful June day in 2002, her words about her memories of days gone by were, "I was attending our old church at the time at 6th and N Streets, where I came in 63 years ago in 1939. That was the Ephesus Seventh-day Adventist Church. It's now the Dupont Park Seventh-day Adventist Church, and I was giving the report for the missionary work that he, Elder Warner, had done for the month. He hadn't even met me, and then, I got up and gave the report." Laughing heartily, Sister Warner stated, "And he said, he said to himself, 'That's going to be my wife.'" Sister Warner further added, "So, then, he met me and started asking people about me, and all the people gave good reports about me, and they all talked about what I was doing in the church. So, we were soon married and were together for 26 wonderful years."

Elder and Sister Warner loved working together and traveled extensively across the continental United States during the 1940's, 1950's, and 1960's. As a devoted Christian, wife, mother, and good friend to many individuals, Sister Warner reiterated, "I didn't marry anymore until October 10, 1943." Then, she said, "We were married by Elder G. E. Peters, who was the first African American worker at the General Conference (GC). The children were grown, and both of them were married." For 26 years, Elder and Sister Warner enjoyed a wonderfully blessed marriage together, and Sister Warner's heart still overflows with love, peace, and joy all these years later.

Many faith-filled experiences were a part of the Warners' many years together. One particular experience came back to Sister Warner like it was just yesterday, and it follows. "My husband was living, and we were here in Washington at that time, and he was pastoring in Cincinnati, Ohio. He was a minister. And so we left here that morning. It was kind of hazy-like. It was December. We got up in those Cumberland Mountains in Maryland, and that snow started to come down. It just looked like it was coming down in sheets, and the windshield wipers were going, but the snow was so heavy. We couldn't see. So, we were headed down a 7 mile mountain, going down, and people were stopped all along the way and couldn't move."

The story continued, "So, we were going down this mountain, and this car, our car, started sliding and there was a big bank of cinders they had there. So, my husband headed the car right into those cinders. We had prayed all the way up there, and finally, we got into Little Washington, Pennsylvania, and I said to my husband, 'I'm going in here to get some isopropyl alcohol or something to put on this windshield to keep the ice from freezing.' So he said, 'You go ahead. I'm going to stay here and pray about it.' And I thought, 'We had said every prayer that could be said.'"

"So anyway," as voiced by Sister Warner, "He (Elder Warner) told the Lord, he said, 'You know Lord, I'm not out here joy riding. I am doing Your work. I have 12 candidates waiting for baptism tomorrow. Now, I don't want to disappoint them. I can't do any more in this snow. If you send rain, I'm not asking You to change the nature of Your weather, but if You send rain, I can make it.'"

In the words of Sister Warner, "We got in the car, went about 2 blocks, and the snow just cut off just like that, and the rain started. Yes, indeed, and we looked at one another and said, 'Thank You Jesus!' Yes sir and we went on in. It took us from 6:00 in the morning to 12:00 that night to get to Cincinnati. It usually didn't take that long. That's right. We'd usually get there about 4:00 in the afternoon, and the church had called because they knew we were having a big baptism the next day, and everybody had started praying, and the Lord carried us through."

Sister Warner, even at over 100 years old, loves to get out of the house, go out and do something, get some fresh air, and just meet other people. As she puts it, "I know that God is in it."

To delve deeper into understanding the kind, loving, and faithful characters of Elder and Sister Warner, let's observe what happened when the conference officials called them one day with a job that only humble servants could have done. She tells the story articulately, memorably, and in her very own calm and mellow way. It follows.

"There was an elder who had been a missionary in Africa, and his wife had been killed. He had also been in the accident. They had 2 children, a boy and a girl. The little girl had gotten hurt too, and they (the Adventist Church) brought them back from Africa. The husband put his daughter in a hospital in New York, but, they (the Conference officials) had this little boy, and they needed somebody to take care of him, and they called me. It looked like every time they needed someone to fill a place, they called me. So I said, 'Well I'm on the road with my husband all the time.' Then I said, 'Wait, I'll ask my husband when he gets home.'"

Unhesitatingly, Sister Warner went on to say, "So when he came in, 'Mr. Fix-It' as I always called him, he said, 'Our brother, he's in trouble, and I think we can help him.' So they brought the child, and he stayed from April that year until February the next year. And he (the father) and the daughter were in the hospital for, I guess, about 3 or 4 months. You see, he got his leg fractured, and she was in a cast from her neck down (her entire body). And I kept the little boy. I guess he was about 6 years old."

Sister Warner further proclaimed, "Now the thing is, when they brought the child here to our home, 9:00 in the morning, he didn't know us, and we didn't know him. The man brought him from the airport. The boy had a grandmother, who lived over in Jersey, and he wanted to go over to his grandmother's, but his grandmother was old."

Sister Warner remembered that the little boy's grandmother "wasn't able to come back and forth to see their father and so forth. So, we talked to him and he just sat in the chair. He wouldn't move. He just sat in the chair. That was about 9:00 in the morning. We got down and prayed around 12:00 and I said, 'Come on and get something to eat,' but he wouldn't eat. He just said, 'I want to go my grandmother's. I want to go to my grandmother's.'"

After prayerfully pondering over this situation with this little boy, Sister Warner said, "If you go to your grandmother's, you won't be able to go see your father and sister. If you stay here, I'll take you whenever you want to go." So anyway, according to Sister Warner's account of this story, the child just sat in the chair. Humbly, she admitted, "If he had cried, I think I could have dealt with it better, but he was just sealed up. He wouldn't do anything. All day, he wouldn't eat."

Then, around 5:00 that afternoon, as she recalled, she said, "Lord, we have prayed, and I just don't know what to do. I'm going in here and talk with him." So she went in there, and in the spirit of agape love, she relentlessly spoke out, "Listen Dwayne, I want you to listen to what I have to say. I say, 'I'm going to run water in the tub, and you will take your bath, and I'm going to give you your dinner, and you're going to bed. Do you understand that?'" Then, she unremittingly continued by saying, "If you don't get up, I'm going to give you the worst spanking you ever had." At that solemn moment, Sister Warner never forgot how Dwayne got right up out of the chair, got his bath, ate his dinner, and went to bed. That was about 6:00 P.M.

After briefly pausing with a smile, Sister Warner unmistakably indicated, "The child didn't wake up until the next day after 1:00 P.M. He was just worn out. I'd been going in there ever so often to see if he was alright. Then, when I went in there at about 1:00 p.m., he had awakened. And he said to me, 'Sister Warner, can you tell me one thing? Why did God take my mother? Why didn't He take me?' I said, 'Now that's something I can not answer, but God can never make a mistake.'"

After Dwayne had rested and talked with Sister Warner, in the words of Tonsa Warner, "Then, he got turned completely around, and we were good friends. He was a nice little fellow after that spell wore off. He was just 6 years old, and we were new people to him, and he didn't know us, but I say now, I'd done everything, and there was nothing else to do. We got down and prayed, 'Lord, help us with this child' because you know, he could have gotten down and gotten sick. That (prayer) is what brought him around."

Sister Warner, along with her husband, worked in the church for years, in different capacities, to get the gospel work done. During one of the interviews, I asked Sister Warner the question, "If I sat in the back of the room as an observer of one of your deaconess meetings, what kinds of things would I hear being said?" Her response to my question is as follows:

"Well, we'd talk about the work and how it could be built up and what the deaconesses do. You see the deaconess is the mother of the church and keep the children under control. Sometimes, the people let the children run all over the church and let the children rip and run in the church and carry on, but you (deaconess) speak to them, and if they (the parents) don't take care of them, you do. Yes, the deaconesses are the mothers of the church, and if a person has a child, or two small children just getting fidgety, the deaconesses just take them out and talk to them. No, you don't see that much anymore. That's about all we'd do and take communion and visit the sick by carrying them food, cleaning up their houses, and helping them in any way we can."

Another office Sister Warner held in the church was that of Sabbath School Superintendent. As Sabbath School Superintendent, Sister Warner said they talked about how they could build the Sabbath School Department up. However, she hadn't been in the church long when she began serving as superintendent. In one particular case, they (the Conference) sent her and her husband to a place where the church was in trouble. All the old officers had to be dismissed, and new officers were installed. So, being a newly installed officer, Sister Warner stated that she took over and learned from the Sabbath School what to do.

"If the people don't want to cooperate with the plan," Sister Warner stressed, "they need to be gotten rid of." It wasn't something one would write home about, but the situation was critical at this church. According to reports they (the Warners) had received, the pastor who was there, at their newly assigned church, kept all the money for himself. He didn't want to send it in to the conference, and so the church was in terrible debt.

So, Sister Warner's husband, Elder Howard David Warner, (known to many as Elder H. D. Warner) whom she affectionately called 'Mr. Fix-it', had been sent up there to help the church get out of trouble. Interestingly, they had been sent to a church where the church officials (for about 20 years) had only been paying interest on the money they had borrowed. As Sister Warner said, "So we got to work, and I worked with the young people. My husband had been Publishing Secretary for the Northeastern Conference. He'd help students during the summer to get them scholarships for school, and he led the world in sales (literature evangelism) that year. So, he was the top man in that, and I'd get out and work with him, and then try to encourage him, you know."

In Sister Warner's narrative voice, "I didn't know too much about his part of the publishing business. I'd just work with the magazines and with the young girls when they would come into the city. I was like the mother to the girls. When they came into town, I'd work with the young girls and young boys to try to help them, and they would listen. These young people would come from Oakwood College in Huntsville, Alabama. After school would close, they would come out from school to make their money for school. They would come here to Washington, DC, or wherever the publishing department would take them."

Regarding college student workers, Sister Warner said, "They would come to New York, and they would work during the summer. Two girls came and were downtown in the bowery, which is a battle ground where it's kind of a rough place and all. You know, every big city has a rough corner in it. So, I said, 'Stay here until we can find a place for you. That's not a place where you would want to work. I worked with these students for 26 years, and I see some of these students now, and they say, 'Sis.

Warner, do you remember me?'" Smiling, Sister Warner replied to me, "I'd forgotten all about them."

Another story that rolled smoothly from Sister Warner's narrative voice told of days at Pine Forge, Pennsylvania, about a half a century ago. She praises God joyfully as she tells it like this. "Now, I was living at Pine Forge, and I knew the young people there. I remember this one little girl, and her father had gotten sick, and she was in Elementary School in Jersey. She wanted to go to Pine Forge so bad, but her father was sick. He was not able to pay the tuition."

To help the young lady mentioned above, Sister Warner stated, "So, I arranged her room and board, and my husband and I decided that we would take her in and let her go to school so she could get her education." She further articulated, "And I say, 'We did it,' and all the young people would come around, and anything they needed, they could come to me for it."

Many memorable moments were recalled, and this brilliant-minded woman of faith shared her stories of days gone by. Therefore, as you continue turning the pages of this document and the pages of history, you might be able to see why Tonsa Fuqua Lavett Warner has agreed to share her story of faith and courage with us. Could it be that she wants us to walk by faith and not by sight, or could it be for thousands of other reasons? Well, Chapter 7 continues with more stories of Sister Warner's journey of faith, and as she prayed during an interview, "Lord, May the words I speak bring somebody closer to You. Bless us and guide us in everything we do and say. This is my prayer. In Your Name, Jesus, Amen."

Tonsa Warner celebrating 100 years of life at her 100th birthday celebration

****

CHAPTER SEVEN

****

"Trust in the LORD with all thine heart; and lean not unto thine own understanding. In all thy ways acknowledge Him, and He shall direct thy paths" (Proverbs 3:5-6, KJV).

Forsaking All I Trust Him

Harlow Lovett (sitting); his wife, Tonsa (standing); and their son, Bunny (age 1) on Harlow's lap

"My daughter was only 4 months old, and my son was almost 2 years old when my first husband (their father, Harlow Lovett) died. So, I waited 20 years before I married again because I didn't want to bring somebody in over my children. I went out and got to work, and my mother was taking care of my children for me until they got up around teenagers (14 or 15), and then I brought them to Washington, DC. We lived in Virginia, but there was no work down there in the country. We had a farm down there, and I came to Washington and worked here."

As Tonsa faithfully trudged on as a single parent for almost 20 years (from 1924 to 1943), she always knew the Lord was with her. To put it in her words, "God has just been so good to me, and I've always tried to do everything I could to help somebody out."

Although this young widow and mother were now faced with the odds against her, she knew, without a doubt that God was and has always been there for her. Even now, as she looks back over the chapters of her life, she still has joy. In her words, "If somebody's in need and I can help them, that gives me more joy than anything. If I can help somebody to make a better life for themselves, then that's what I like."

During the good times and the times of disappointment, Sister Tonsa Lavett Warner held her head up and continued to know that God was and is still her "All and All." Every now and then, Sister Warner would talk about the prejudicial attitudes of the early 1900's and beyond. At one point, I asked her the question, "What do you think went through people's minds to move them to make post-slavery laws after slavery was outlawed in America?" In a hesitatingly humorous but stern way, she gave the reply, "I don't know." She continued commenting, "The thing that kind of puzzles me sometimes is we were all born the same way. Why do we have to be so different? Why would a person want to kill somebody else because they weren't their color or something? That's right. That's right." Many questions will go unanswered for now, but we can continue searching anyway. Wouldn't you say?

On October 10, 1943, as was mentioned in the previous chapter, Sister Tonsa Nella Fuqua Lavett married Elder Howard David "H.D." Warner. For the next 26 years, the Warners would leave their legacy of agape love and faithfulness upon the minds, hearts, and lives of thousands of souls needing it.

Tonsa's words ring out, "The biggest joy you can get out of life is what you can do for others. You feel good if you can help somebody along life's way, just a kind word, a smile, or something can bring joy to some other heart. If a person's in trouble, you try to help them. You think of others more than you think of yourself. If you see someone who looks like they're into something, you speak a kind word or something, and tell them the way to go, to turn from that (the wrong way) and go the other way (the right way)."

An example of Elder and Sister Warner helping someone along life's way follows in the narrative voice of Sister Tonsa Warner. "Well, people are going to say something about everything, whether it's good or bad or in between. They're going to say it. My husband and I got married in 1943. In 1944, they (the Conference) sent us to Cincinnati in a split church. They weren't sending the tithes or anything to the conference. They were keeping the money. Split meant divided. Some of the members believed withholding the tithes was right, and other members went with the conference (believed in returning a faithful tithe). They were fighting against one another."

Certainly, this was a delicate and very sensitive situation the Warners found themselves in with the church being split like that. She went on to explain, "Then, the pastor pulled out, and they went out and got (started) another church for the pastor and not the conference. He went out there, and my husband told him, 'When it comes time for your sustenance, you won't get a dime because you pulled away from the body.'"

In Sister Warner's words, as she remembered these challenges, they "had a time there, but the Lord worked it all out." She continued by saying, "We went there, and on Sabbath (Saturday) morning, their group would sit on one side of this big church, and the other group would sit on the other side. While my husband was preaching, this man (the other pastor) would say, 'Amen' and nobody else would. My husband would invite him to come up on the rostrum, but he wouldn't come up."

Sister Warner remembered how the pastor who was supposed to have been gone when they arrived was still in the parsonage and wouldn't leave. He wouldn't move. He just stayed there. In her words, "I don't know what was wrong with him. The devil got in him I guess, and so, we went on and found out that the school had been closed. So, we got to working. I tried to work with the older people. They were difficult. So, I said I'm going to work with the young people, and we got with the young people and went out every Sunday and solicited (funds to get the church out of debt)."

Sister Warner went on to express, "We paid the church off. The church had been standing there for 20 years. The only thing they had been paying on the church was the interest on the loan. So, we paid the church off and opened up the school again. The people had kept the money for themselves and did what they wanted to do with it.

The last day the old pastor was at the church, we had a baptism. There were about 20 people to be baptized, and he (the ex-pastor) asked my husband to baptize him." In other words, on his last day at this church, the ex-pastor had made the decision to go down in the baptismal pool himself and rededicate his life to Jesus Christ and be re-baptized by Elder H. D. Warner. What a day of rejoicing it must have been!

Sister Warner recalled that the old pastor would never move out of the parsonage, and it was 14 months (after coming to their new church) before they could find a place of their own. As Sister Warner said, "My husband had gone to talk with him (the ex-pastor). He liked my husband, but he was one of those people that liked to do what they wanted to do. And he said to my husband one day, 'You're the only man that could have come into this place and got things done the way you did.' He also said, 'Even your enemies like you.' Well, we didn't have any enemies because we hadn't done anything to anybody."

In her own quiet way, Sister Warner stated, "We just went to where the conference sent us. So, we stayed there and got all the debts paid off, and the teachers hadn't been paid in years, and we paid them off and gave them their money. We stayed there 3½ years, and the church was out of debt when we left. We worked hard there." She further stated, "Five (5) years were the limit at one (1) church (during that era), and then they (the conference) moved you on. If they had a church that needed help, they'd send my husband to that church to build it up."

While Elder and Sister Warner were in Cincinnati, Sister Warner said the publishing work (literature evangelism) had gone down, and they sent her husband out there to get things straight. So he had to come back and straighten that out. She said, "He was Mr. Fix-it. When anything went wrong, they sent him. He could work with anybody. They even had to get all new officers for the church, and we just prayed for the situation. One day we were sitting at the table and my husband began to weep, and I said, 'Honey, you're doing all you can. Don't let it get you down.' I said, 'Just keep on praying, and the Lord will answer your prayers.' And we came out of there in flying colors, and everything was left in order."

Having been a pastor's wife for 26 years, Sister Warner declared, "Pastors are under a lot of pressure, and it's hard work, yes indeed. Many people think the pastor's job is easy, but it's not. You have different minds to deal with. You try to point everybody in the right direction, and some of them don't want to listen, and that's the way that goes, but you just do your best, and the Lord will do the rest. That's what he did for us. Time is valuable, but when you're doing good, that's alright."

"I've been in every state in the union except Hawaii and Alaska," Sister Warner said to me. "We traveled by car all over the United States because my husband worked for the conference. The last evening we had General Conference (GC) sessions in Detroit, Michigan, my husband wanted to go, but he wasn't well. The doctor said, 'Don't take him up there because if you take him up there, you'll bring him back in a box. It would be too much for him.'" This was very difficult for both Elder and Sister Warner because of their extensive travels over the years.

So, one day Sister Warner said to her husband, "Honey, would you really like to go?" He said, "Yes." So, she said, "Yes, we'll trust in the Lord, and let His Will be done." Sister Warner reported, "We got in the car in New York and went up to Ottawa, Canada, and we stayed up there 3 days. Then, we came back to Detroit and stayed there 10 days, and after the conference was over with, we went all the way back across Canada to Toronto, left there and came back there to Portland, Maine, and came back over to Detroit. And you know he never got under the steering wheel. I drove every inch of the way (laughing). That's been 33 years."

Elder and Sister Warner had a marvelous time traveling cross country and to Canada for 2 to 3 weeks, although, his health was still not the best. By the way, Elder Warner lived an additional fifteen years after he and Sister Warner returned from their cross country travels (which included the GC sessions in Detroit). With twinges of sadness in her voice, during one of our interview sessions in June 2002, Sister Warner expressed, "He's gone now. That will be 33 years in July (2002)."

Elder Warner had been given a church (in New York) because he had been on the road a lot in the publishing work (literature evangelism). So, they (the Conference) said they would give him a church to pastor so he wouldn't have to do too much traveling. Sister Warner admitted, "He hadn't been doing too well (with his health). So, we were going to church one morning, and I said, 'Honey, why don't you have one of the elders to speak today because you have four of them sitting up there on the rostrum?' Well, we went on to Sabbath School. He had taken (read) his text (during the 11:00 hour) and he dropped right down (fell to the floor). My husband died right in the pulpit."

Sister Warner reminisced, "Yes sir. I remember how he would be around the house (sometimes downstairs), and I would call him and he didn't answer me, and I would stop calling him because I knew he was praying. He would be at the window praying. I'd tip downstairs, and he'd be at the window praying. He was a prayer warrior, oh yes, Lord, indeed."

Sister Warner further remembers, "After my husband died in 1969, in New York, in July, after he passed, everything just went out for me. I said, 'Well, ain't no sense in me staying up here by myself. We were buying a home, but I thought about moving back to Washington, DC, and getting an apartment. So, I told my son, and I called the lawyer and real estate agent, and he (the real estate agent) wanted to take it (buy my home) exclusively. He didn't want anyone else to take it. I wanted to have more than one prospective buyer. So, I said, 'The lawyer and I will take it over.'"

Her story continued, "My husband died in July, and it was now January (1970), and my neighbor next door was young, and he was on the police force, and he said, 'Sister Warner, I know someone who would love to live out here. You want me to ask them?' I said, 'You can do that. Sure!'"

Sister Warner remembered the story about selling her house as if it was yesterday. According to her recollection, "The woman (and her husband) came to the door (Sister Warner's house in New York) and stepped in the door (house), and she (the wife) said, 'I want this house.' I just turned it over, and I said, 'Lord, you know I want to get away. There is nothing. It means nothing up here for me now. I wanted to get away and come back to family."

So, the house was sold to the first woman (family) that came along, and the Lord has always answered so many prayers for Sister Warner. She continued her story by saying, "This was St. Auburn, New York. So, I called my son and told him when I was leaving. So, when I was moving out, the people (buyers) were moving in. He (my son) came that day (that I sold my house), and I was just low, looked like my spirits were just down. I was selling my home and leaving by myself you know. So,

I left to go see the lawyer and when I came back, the lady said a man had been by to see me. She acted like she didn't know who it was. I said alright, and at that time, a knock came to the door, and it was my son, and I said, 'Boy come in here!' I was so happy to see him because I had never felt so low in all my life. God really does know how to send someone when we need them. So, we sold the home."

I have been in this house (in Washington, DC) for 32 years. I was going to get an apartment, and he (my son, Bunny) said, "No, you're coming to my house. Nobody's in that house but the two of us (Bunny and his wife), and there's plenty of room. So, you come and live with us. Then, my daughter's husband passed (not long after that). Then, my son's wife passed, and it was only the two of us living here. So, he asked his sister (Violet) to come live with us. So, now it's the three of us. See how God will work things out? So, I think the greatest joy in my life now is being with the two of them – considering I didn't have the opportunity to be with them (live with them) when they were small."

Through it all, Sister Tonsa Lavett Warner has maintained her faith in God. I asked her the brief question "What does faith mean to you?" She quickly replied, "It means everything. Yes, if you can't work it out, just leave it in His (God's) hands. Say, 'Lord, take it; it's too hard for me.' Yes, He (God) can work it out, not me." As her story continues in Chapter 8, we will learn what Tonsa Nella Fuqua Lavett Warner's life is like as a senior of over 100 years of age.

****

CHAPTER EIGHT

****

"But the fruit of the Spirit is love, joy, peace, longsuffering, gentleness, goodness, faith, meekness, temperance: against such there is no law" (Galatians 5:22-23, KJV).

Healthy & Happy At 101 Years of Age

Tonsa Nella Fuqua Lavett Warner's life has truly been a journey of faith, hope, and love, from sharing precious moments with her grandmother, Lucinda, as a little girl, to smiling, styling, and profiling with her first great, great, great grandson, Anthony, as a centurion. Tonsa's grandmother, Lucinda, was from Roanoke, Virginia, where her mother, Nellie, was born. Furthermore, her grandmother was half Native American and half White American.

According to Tonsa's report on her grandmother, "The older people didn't talk to the children. When the grown people came in the house, the children had to get out, which I thought was unfair in a way because they weren't teaching the children life, but that was grown people talk, and you weren't in it. She lived with us." Her name was Lucinda Otey, and her husband was Edmond Otey, a Native American whom she met and married on a slave plantation, as mentioned earlier. He (Edmond Otey) was Tonsa's grandfather, who passed away before she was born.

Surely, there have been so much fellowship and so many family and friends along the way. It is a tough task to tell it all. After 100 plus years of glorious living, Tonsa Nella Fuqua Lavett Warner gracefully and eloquently shares her 100th birthday with family and friends. She takes us on a tour of this awesome day and talks about how faith in God influenced her every move. The story is as follows:

During our interview session on May 27, 2002, Sister Warner talked about her 100th birthday. "My birthday at the church? You see, I had planned to drive my self to church. I told my sister I wanted to borrow her car to drive my own self to church. I didn't want anybody to go with me. I just wanted to feel free, at 100 years old, driving my own self to church. Yes, and the children found it out, and I had said, 'Don't say anything.'"

She continued, "So, some way or another, they found it out, and they had planned something else. So, we got together, and I had to give in, and I said, 'Well, I'll just go with what you all want to do. I will do it. So, my grandson lives over in Virginia, and so, we all had to wait for him to come, and we'd all go together, and we were standing out front waiting, and what they had planned – he would bring the limousine and carry us all to church."

With a sparkle in her eyes, Sister Warner exclaimed, "So, he drove us, and that was the biggest surprise in my whole set up! That was on

April 20, 2002. That was on the Sabbath. The Chancel Choir at Dupont Park SDA Church didn't sing my song that week, but they sang it the following week. My favorite song is 'Just for Me.' That is the way the day went."

Further expounding on her 100th birthday, Sister Tonsa Warner concluded, "Then, we went to Major's house. Major Evans had my family and my friends there for dinner that day. Then, after that, we all came home together, but it was a grand day. As I say, 'that was the best day I ever had – after my wedding day!'"

During the month of May 2002, Sister Warner had a big 100th birthday celebration at the General Conference (GC) in Silver Spring, Maryland, and as she phrased it, "It was beautiful. That was beautiful. Everything just went beautiful. Elder Thompson was an old friend. I remember him from his first church. He didn't want to stop talking. No, he didn't want to stop talking, but he could go on and on and on."

Sister Warner shared a wonderful story about her first meeting with Elder and Sister Thompson, and it follows. "I was visiting my brother in Montgomery, West Virginia, which was about 35 miles away, and I asked my brother if there was a bus I could get down to Charleston because I wanted to go to church. He said, 'Nah, but my neighbor goes down everyday. He (the neighbor) is a principal of a school down there, and he'll take you.' So, he called him, and he (my brother) said, 'He (the principal) would be glad to take you down, but he wouldn't be down there all day because he had to come back.' So, I said, 'I'll get to Sabbath School.' So, he (the principal) carried me down, and I went to Sabbath School."

Sister Warner stated that when she had to leave, after having sat in Elder Thompson's Sabbath School class, he (Elder Thompson) said to her, "Well, I'm sorry you have to leave," but I said to him, "Well, I got to get my ride back to Montgomery." In Sister Warner's words, "And that's the way the day went. That's the first day his wife had come in. She was a new bride. They had just gotten married the week before."

Sister Warner recalled, "She (Elder Thompson's wife) came in on that Sabbath day – beautiful. I remember all those years ago, ah hah. And I remember the dress she had on. She had on a china blue satin dress and hat to match. And so, I said to him, 'I'm sorry I have to leave.' So I had to go back to where the man was going to pick me up. So he (Elder Thompson) said, 'Is somebody taking you?' I said, 'No,' then he said to his elder, 'You take over until I get back.' So, he carried me to where I had to meet the man to go back to Montgomery. That was my first meeting with the Thompsons, and we've been friends ever since."

I asked Sister Warner to connect faith in God to everything that happened that day from the time she got up on her 100th birthday 'til the time she retired that evening. Her story is one of faith and her reply was one of faith, and it is as follows: "That's something that comes from within you. You think about a thing, and you pray over it, and sometimes you think God doesn't hear you, but He hears. He sends it in His time not yours. I may want it tomorrow, but He may not be ready for it until next week. So, we just wait on Him. We wait on the Lord and be of good courage, and He will direct our path."

During our interviews, Sister Warner eloquently and articulately shared her life story with me without hesitation. Having known her for over a decade, I have noticed her love for brightly colored clothing, with her favorites being red and white. Even at her 100th birthday celebration, she was gracefully styling her red and white attire, with hat and shoes to match. Oh, by the way, her son and her daughter also stepped out in red and white, and they looked marvelous.

I asked Sister Warner during one of our interview sessions to tell me reasons red and white were her favorite colors. Her response was, "I love bright colors, white, red, green, and yellow, okay, and I love colors. I don't like dark clothes. I don't know why. Well, my mother, that's the way she did. She'd always put light colors on us, and I guess I grew up with it." My question to you dear reader is, "What do you think?"

To add more about color, Sister Warner expressed more of her views about colors after I admired her moo moo (big colorful dress) while chatting with her one day. She commented, "Oh my sister bought this for me when she went to Hawaii. It has all the colors (so many different colors) in it: lime green, purple, pink, orange, yellow, and so many more."

One question that I couldn't resist asking Sister Warner was, "How do you feel being 100?" Her answer was clearly and simply stated, "I feel the same. I haven't changed. All I can say is 'God has been good to me.' I'm able to do for myself and all of that, and it's so many people younger than myself and can't do for themselves. I never went in for a whole lot of exercising." I therefore came to conclude that the bottom line is God has sustained her. Wouldn't you say?

Another very interesting topic of discussion that we had was on vegetarianism. Sister Warner has been a vegetarian for over 55 years. She loves vegetables and all kinds of fruit as well as the vegetarian products that have a similar texture to meat. In her words, "You can prepare the vegetarian ingredients just like you do meats. You can fry it and bake it, ah hah. I think that food has a lot to do with good health."

What do you think has sustained you? Do you think vegetarianism is a part of it? This twofold question elicited the following response. "I think so, ah hah. I've had pretty good health. I had an operation (on my knee) some years ago, but I came through it. When did I stop eating meat? Well, we were eating one Christmas. I don't remember the year now (it's been over 50 years ago). A friend of ours where we were living in Pottstown, Pennsylvania, invited us to Christmas dinner. And they had this turkey, and something about this turkey just didn't taste right. So when we left, I said, 'I don't think I want anymore turkey or chicken,' and we (my husband and I) stopped right there. We cut the meat off and never ate it again. I have been a vegetarian for over 50 years and an Adventist for 63 years (as of 2002)."

Elder and Sister Warner both felt the same way about that dinner and their determination to stop eating meat. They were born just 2 days apart (Sis. Warner on April 20, 1902 and Elder Warner on April 22, 1902), and sometimes Sister Warner would go to say something to Elder Warner, and he would say, 'Wait a minute. Let me get mine in first. It would be the same thing I was going to say to him,' according to Sister Warner's recall of events.

As Sister Warner spoke about her favorite foods, it was obvious that she does her best to eat foods that encourage good health. Here is how she expounded on the subject of 'favorite foods.' "I eat any foods like vegetables and fruit. Fruit is my favorite meal. I love all types of fruit. I like all vegetables. I don't know any vegetable that I don't like. I don't like one better than the other one, but I just love vegetables like sweet potatoes, corn, and all of that. I like corn on the cob or cut off the cob with a little butter on it. I like proteins and soy bean products and lots of things like that. I don't eat the soy products everyday. I like the raw vegetables and the raw fruit. I can eat things like that, coleslaw and salads, with nice sliced tomatoes, with lettuce cut up. I can enjoy that."

Having grown up eating different meats, Sister Warner made a conscious decision to become a vegetarian as a middle-aged adult. Therefore, she clearly enunciated, "I try to tell the people that they shouldn't eat it. Even though she ate meat and survived as a child and young adult, she now declares, "You shouldn't have to kill something to eat it to keep you alive." Because of the controversial nature of this issue, Tonsa also verbalized, "but they (people) don't want to hear it. So, you just pass that over and let that go."

"Well," she went on to say, "Let me tell you why we ate the meat anyway. Before the flood, people weren't supposed to kill to eat because they had the vegetation of the earth. So, when the flood came, it destroyed all of the vegetation. There was nothing left. Nothing was left to eat. So they had to kill the animals (see Leviticus 11 and Deuteronomy 14) in order to have something to eat. That's where that meat eating came in. After the vegetation grew back, the people were supposed to go back to eating from the earth (see Genesis 1:29), but all of us didn't. I don't miss the meat. I never was a big meat eater anyway. I ate it, all kinds of meat, everything that walked. If I wanted it, I ate it until I found out different."

In regard to health and foods, Sister Warner added, "I don't eat a lot of sweets. I never cared for a lot of sweets. I'll have a piece of cake or pie once in awhile, but having to have something sweet all the time, I don't have an appetite for it."

During our time together, Sister Warner shared many smiles, and she told me story after story. There are many results of genuinely smiling, but as Sister Warner stated, "If you smile at a person, they think you care. They feel you're friendly. A smile will turn away wrath. It just makes you feel good when a person smiles at you." One particular story, I will share with you now in the narrative voice of Tonsa Warner.

"One day I was selling some books, and I looked at this man, who looked like he was mad with the world, and I asked him if he wanted to buy some books, and he snapped at me, 'I don't want to buy nothing!' So I said, 'Thank you very much. I'm sorry.' And I turned around and went to the next person, and the man went on down to the corner and turned around and came back to me and said, 'Lady I'm sorry for the way I spoke to you. I had no business speaking to you like that. Please forgive me.' And he said, 'I'll pay for the magazine, but I don't want it.' And then he said, 'You know why I came back? It's because you smiled.'"

According to Tonsa, "You know sometimes a smile will turn away wrath. If we just speak to a person that's down because it's only the grace of God that will keep you on your feet. That's right. You never scorn a person. I don't care how bad they look or what they have or whatever – their hair could be all ruffled or whatever – you just say a little prayer for them, yes."

As this chapter comes to a close, I can truly say that God has tremendously blessed Sister Tonsa Warner. In celebrating 100 years of living a good life, Sister Warner puts it like this, "I just felt good and happy being surprised that way. That was the only surprise I had. Then when the limousine turned the corner, I said, 'Ah hah, this is my surprise.' Well, I just felt that God was so good that I had made those 100 years, and I just couldn't give Him enough thanks. Furthermore, "God made me a woman and a lady, and that's what I wanted to be, not living the rough life – drinking, smoking, and cussing. I have plenty of friends who have lived clean lives, but if you can just give them a word to encourage people to keep going and live right and go in the right direction. I have helped a lot of young people turn around and see they're going the wrong way." What a testimony to the effects of healthy and joyful living! Now, let's read more of Sister Warner's story in Chapter 9, which is entitled, 'Great is God's Faithfulness.'

Tonsa Warner (age 100) sitting; and her sister, Taqua Trescott (age 88), standing, Christmas Dinner 2002

```
*************************************
```

CHAPTER NINE

```
*************************************
```

Therefore we also, since we are surrounded by so great a cloud of witnesses, let us lay aside every weight, and the sin which so easily ensnares us, and let us run with endurance the race that is set before us, looking unto Jesus, the author and finisher of our faith, who for the joy that was set before Him endured the cross, despising the shame, and has sat down at the right hand of the throne of God" (Hebrews 12:1-2, NKJV).

Great is God's Faithfulness

Born in 1902, Tonsa Nella Fuqua Lavett Warner's firsthand historical sketch includes the following events that crowd her life and times: the invention of the automobile, the radio coming on the scene, astounding inventions of the television and many other technological gadgets, surviving Jim Crow Laws and racism at its worst, World War I, Women's Rights, the Roaring 20's, the Great Depression,

World War II, the Korean War, the Vietnam War, Civil Rights, the 1970's and 1980's, the fall of Communism and Apartheid, the 1990's, Y2K, and the devastating effects of 9-11 and beyond.

Yet, she never worried about any of the events that came and was gone because of God's great faithfulness to her. As she shared, "I always thought about Booker T. Washington and the other big men back during that time and how they got their education when we didn't have schools like the White people had. I guess you have to be born with it in you and say, 'I'm going to do something,'" and do something she did. She has kept the faith and always believed that God was with her through the ups and downs, the smiles and the frowns.

Great is God's faithfulness to you and to me. As a woman of color from start to finish, Tonsa Nella Fuqua Lavett Warner has allowed her faith in God to get her through life. She has always known, too, that God has been and still is even more faithful to her than she could ever imagine. Reflecting on her years as a young widow doing her best to make it, her words echo, "Just made up my mind that this is my life, and I am going to be the best that I am. I was just blessed to get in with (work for) people who were nice to me since I had children."

"The White lady I worked for had a girl and her sister had a boy about the same age as my children, and they would give me the clothes they had for their children. I mean real clothes, not no 10 Cents Store something. And that's the way I kept them (my children) dressed so nicely all the time. They were always the best dressed children. That was a blessing there. And I lived in the house and didn't have to pay rent, and I got my food free. So what you made was yours because you didn't have any bills to pay," which we can all say is truly a blessing.

Having been a devoted and loyal Seventh-day Adventist for 63 years, I asked Sister Warner to tell me about the Sabbath Day and what it means to her. She reverently revealed, "It just means all to me. When I miss going to church, it seems to me as if I've missed a blessing. I get out here and I try to get to church on time, but after I sold my car (at 99 years old), now I have to depend on other people. I am at home and ready to go at 8:00 A.M. because I want to be there for teachers' meeting (which starts at 8:30 A.M. on Saturday). And every place I've gone, I just went to church."

She further expounded, "I'll tell you what . . . . I was a great dancer before I knew about Seventh-day Adventists. You see, my mother didn't believe in dancing. Christians don't dance, and I think that had something to do with it (me stopping dancing) because that was the joy I had in life – dancing. I didn't care for playing cards and all that kind of stuff – like most young people get into. All I wanted to do was get on the dance floor and have a good time. Then, it would come back to me that my mother said, 'Christians don't dance!' Then I'd go to different churches, and I'd go to the dance halls and see some of the good deacons at the dance hall too."

Sister Warner remembered some of the people that encouraged her when she first joined the Adventist church. "Oh yes," she said, "the people that were there when I came into the church – all of them are just about gone (deceased). I knew so many – the Dobsons, the Smiths, I can't call all of their names right now, but I remember them. Yes, Sister Anderson was there, she and her family, and Sister McAllister and Sister Booker. I can see their faces (in my mind) but I can't think of their names right now."

Words of faith rang from Sister Warner's narrative voice, "But I say I'm going to 105, but whatever the Will of God. My grandfather lived to be 104, and nobody has gone beyond that. So, somebody has to go past 104. That's right. So, I think it's going to be me. It's marvelous to make it to 100."

This great woman of faith expressed, "I feel I've been blessed, just blessed. When I go to church, I feel good when I walk in the church, knowing that Christ is there with you, and your family, your church family, everybody is so loving and kind. 'Just for Me' is my favorite song. Wasn't that beautiful? It is. He (Minister of Music) said he was going to give me the tape of it (the song, 'Just for Me' being sung by the Chancel Choir)."

Faith in God is strongly connected to Sister Warner's decision making from day to day because she realized long ago how great God's faithfulness was and is to her. "Well, I just pray in the morning, 'Lord give me strength for this day, and guide me and lead me in any way you want me to go, and anybody I can help, let me help them in any way possible if I can help them. I pray all the time. I just pray all during the day. I just stop and say a prayer. I just say, 'Lord, be my guide in everything I do,' and my sister always says to me that every time I get in the car, I pray. Yes, I pray, 'Lord, you do the driving. I'm just here.' And I get in her car and say, 'Lord help her and guide and lead her.' Anybody's car I get in, I don't pray out loud all the time 'cause everybody doesn't want to hear it, but I just pray, 'Lord take us safely and bring us back.'"

Tonsa's words of wisdom continued, "Well I think everything I do, I just have faith to believe that His Will, not mine, be done. Sometimes, we want things that are not going to benefit us. But, if it's His Will, whatever you ask for, He'll give it to you in His way, maybe not the way I want it or ask for it. It's got to be His Will."

According to Sister Warner, "He (God) just has led me in things I never thought of. You see good things would come to me, and the thing that makes you feel good is that somebody on the street may walk up to you and say, 'I'm hungry, or would you give me a dime, or would you give me this?' and I'll give it to them. And I just love helping people in every way I can – clothes and everything else. Even before I was a Seventh-day Adventist, I'd always help everybody I could help. It was just me. It was part of my life – giving. I always did whatever I could do to bring joy to someone else."

Story after story was shared during our interviews, especially stories about helping others and the joy it brings. Sister Warner also spoke of qualities of being a Christian, which are: gentle speaking, silent when necessary, forgiving, smiling, prayerfulness, taking people in (though you must be careful today), cooking for and feeding others, respectfulness, faithfulness (to God and spouse), and non-violence.

In her very own special way, Sister Warner told stories of compassion and support to those in need. "Years ago, I'd pick people up when I'd see them standing at the bus stop and take them where they had to go, but now you're afraid to do that. For you don't know who you're picking up. You can't do that now (pick up strangers & give them a ride)."

Tonsa continued, "I remember one day I was at 15th and U Streets, NW, Washington, DC. This was years ago, and I stopped there at the light, and this old White woman came up to my car and said, 'Would you take me to Chevy Chase, MD?' and I said, 'No. I'm sorry, but I don't have time,' and I looked at her, and she looked just like my grandmother. So I said, 'Alright, I'll take you.' So, I took her to Chevy Chase, and she lived out there in a big home in Chevy Chase where it was the roughest part of the city. So, she said, 'You know what, I'd like to have some cornbread. Do you make cornbread? I'd like to have some cornbread and fried chicken with some buttermilk.'"

Smiling, Tonsa further stated, "So, my sister was living at the time, and I came back and got the chicken, cooked the cornbread, and carried it out there to her. And she lived out there in a big home, and she was so grateful that I had fixed that and brought it out there to her (laughed). Now I lived over here on Ames Street, NE, (Washington, DC), and I told her where I lived, and she got on the bus, and came out here one day to see me, but I wasn't at home but at work."

Another story Sister Warner told follows: "Today you look at them and wonder if they're telling the truth, and if I have it, I don't open my pocketbook (if I have some money). A man came up to me at the market one day and said, 'Lady I'm so hungry. I haven't had anything to eat since yesterday. Won't you give me 50 cents?' He looked like he was really hungry. So, I gave him a dollar, and he just appreciated it so much. Now, I don't know if he was going out to buy liquor or what."

In another episode of hospitality, Sister Warner commented, "I came out of the bank one day, and this man said, 'Can you give me 25 cents to help me get something to eat?' I said, 'okay,' and I gave it to him. Then, he said, 'You didn't ask me what I was going to do with it,' and I said, 'that's between you and your God. I'm giving it to you. Now you use it right.' He said, 'Oh my Lord!' I don't know what was wrong with him. I think he wanted a drink or something."

Sister Warner continued, "But you just can't help people today. You're afraid. You pick them up in your car, and the first thing, they find you dead somewhere. People will just come in your house and kill you for nothing. You just don't want to help people in today's times because your heart could be in the right place, but you don't know if theirs is in the right place or not."

The Mother's Day after her 100th birthday (May 2002), Sister Warner was delighted to be in the company of wonderful people as they celebrated Mother's Day with her. Here's her story, "Today, a friend of my son took all of us out to a Mothers' Day brunch at Bolling Air Force Base. It was about 12 or 13 of us – his mother and his sister and her daughter and some others. We had lunch out there today. Then, my son brought us home after driving around downtown (Washington, DC). I hadn't been down there in a long time, and I enjoyed the day. It was a beautiful day. I'm the kind of person who loves to get out, just go, just get out and do something. Don't stay in the house all day, get out and get some fresh air and see other people."

Then, Sister Warner began reflecting on days spent with her parents. In her narrative voice, "My father passed in 1932 when we were grown, and my mother passed in 1962. My father passed when he was in his 60's. He was still a young man. Well, he was not an old person."

"My mother was 88 when she died," stated Sister Tonsa Warner. Before her mother passed, Tonsa remembers how God was constantly working in Mrs. Fuqua's life. Tonsa explained, "She (my mother) got sick. We carried her to a hospital in Charlottesville, VA. She had cancer. That's what they had diagnosed her with, and the doctors said there was nothing they could do. It was no sense in leaving her there because she was not well. After five days, we carried her home."

The story continued being told, "Everyday, we thought it would be the last day (of mother's life). They had 3 doctors come everyday to give her this morphine to ease her pain. She called me to her and said, 'Don't have the doctors to come here anymore. Just let them stay at home. I'm going to put my hand in the hands of Dr. Jesus. If He sees fit to heal me, I'll get up. If not, I want to go in my right mind.'"

Tonsa declared, "You know from that date, the next day, she (my mother) was feeling better, and they gave her 5 days to live. The next day she was feeling a little better. Then, after awhile, she could get out of the bed and walk to the kitchen. My mother got up and lived 32 years, another 32 years. Then, when they (the doctors) found out that she didn't die, they wanted her to come back (to the hospital) so they could see what happened. And she said, 'No, because God healed me!' She put her faith in His (God's) hands."

When Mrs. Nellie Fuqua passed away, Tonsa was in New York and came down to Washington, DC, (after her sister called her). They had put her mother in the hospital, and Tonsa would stay with her mother around the clock (many times to 3:00 in the morning). Her mother's last words were, 'I'm talking to Dr. Jesus.' Tonsa recalls, "The hospital called and told us about 10 minutes after we had just left the hospital (and arrived at my sister's house) that Mother had passed."

Tonsa's love and respect for her mother has stayed with her all of her life, and as she so nicely shared, "I believe in praying because we were taught that from our mother. She was a Christian lady. She believed in God, and she put him first in everything we would do or what she would do. We were brought up in a Christian home, and that's what did it. I think I was the most obedient child. They always say that I'm just saying that, but I just felt good when I did things my mother told me to do."

Many memorable moments have been spent with Sister Warner during interviews, enjoying lunch, chatting on the phone, driving down the road, worshipping at church, feasting at her birthday celebration, and visiting and fellowshipping with her sister and other family members. Over and over again, Sister Warner reminded me of God's great faithfulness to her. So, as the next chapter of this book unfolds, please keep on enjoying the serenity of reading the story of this faithful centurion, who doesn't mind calling it like she sees it. Inclusive also in the next chapter are more words of wisdom for such a time as this. Please prayerfully enjoy!

****

CHAPTER TEN

****

"Wisdom is the principal thing; therefore get wisdom: and with all thy getting get understanding" (Proverbs 4:7, KJV).

Words of Wisdom for Today's Times

Where will I be at 100 years of age? Where will you be at the age of 100? What will I be doing? What will you be doing? Will either of us be licensed to drive anywhere? Will we be actually able (physically or emotionally) to drive ourselves anywhere? Well, that is not an issue of concern right now. However, it is possible because anything is possible. What do you think?

Sister Tonsa Lavett Warner, a woman of 101 years of age, makes it very exciting as she speaks about her driving days. She even drove herself to church on her 101st birthday, and said, "I felt free." During one of our last interviews, I asked her to take me through the steps (verbally) she took to drive and get her first drivers license. Here is her story, as only Tonsa could tell it.

"Everybody's car I got in I would watch what they (each driver) did. I was determined that I was going to learn how to drive. I would have gotten the people to teach me, but I didn't have the money for that. So, I would watch everybody's car I'd get in. I must have been about 17 when I started watching people drive. One day I was watching this man when he drove up to the house, and he said, 'You can't drive outside,' and I said, 'I bet I can.' Then, he said, 'If you can drive this car, you can have it.' He was just talking you know. So, I got in there and drove the car around the block, but I didn't get it (didn't get the car). So, I went down and got my license (at 18 years old)."

She went on commenting, "You know you have to know the stops and signs, and it was not lights like there are today. It was right here in the city (Washington, DC). When the police had taken me out for my test (because the police took everybody out for their driving test back then), we had to go down and register, and then they'd take you out and test you. We had to go to the 13th Street Hill, and that's where they'd take you and test you and see if you could park there. I couldn't park that car. So I said to the police, 'You make me nervous. Why don't you get out of this car so I can park it?' So, he got out of the car, and I parked it, and I got my license."

As Sister Warner recalled, "Getting my license must have been in 1920. They'd give you a regular license for a year, and you'd go back every year. I think it was $2 or $3 – something like that. If you never had a license, the police would take you around the block to test your driving and in the traffic to see how you drive and handle the car."

According to what's going on today, Sister Warner explained, "So, now you can get your license for 3 years. I don't think these red light cameras are fair to the drivers. The people shouldn't go through the red lights, but youngsters are always in a big hurry. They started this about 2 years ago, and it's just unfair."

Sister Warner went on to say, "I still have my license for 2 more years (until 2004), and I can go down and get it renewed and have an eye test and a doctor's test and all of that, and I can get it (driver's license). Getting another car, I don't think so. I won't bother (laughing). I'll be about 103 by then. No, I'm not going to bother it. As long as my mind is not fuzzy, and my reflexes are good, I love to drive. It doesn't bother me."

Constantly engaging her faith in God, Sister Warner reflected, "I sold my car in July 2001. With all these young children driving out here, my children said, 'Get rid of that car. You don't need it.' So, I said, 'I'm going to make this a subject of prayer,' and I said, 'Lord, you show me what to do with this car.' So, I left it in His hands."

Sister Warner's words continued to flow eloquently, "So, my sister was in the hospital, and she came out and stayed a week with me. So, the nurse came to visit her, and my sister, Taqua, told the nurse how old I was, and she also told her that I was still driving. So, when I went to the door to let her (the nurse) out, she said, 'Is that your car?' And I said, 'Yes.' And I said, 'Do you want to buy it?' She said, 'Do you mean it?' And I said, 'Yes.' And the Lord sold the car right there. The woman never turned the switch on or anything. The Lord just guided it. He sold it for me."

Certainly, I have read about the faith of our fathers and mothers in the history books. I have also seen faith at work in the lives of others throughout the generations, especially people of Color. Furthermore, I have experienced faith in God for myself, particularly while writing my dissertation, which dealt with the role of faith in God in administrative decision making. However, it is an honor and privilege to write this story about Tonsa Warner's journey of faith.

Not even being half of Sister Tonsa Warner's age, it has truly been an exciting journey of faith for me to hear, transcribe, analyze, and interpret the wealth of information received from this sensational centurion during the many hours of our interview sessions. Her words rang out clearly, "I know God has always brought me through. I can just look back and see how God has led me, and I was never hungry or out of a dime. Money was short sometimes, but I made it. That was Him (God) that did it. No, I didn't know much about the Great Depression because I had food to eat, 2 or 3 cents in my pocket, and if something would come up, I had 2 or 3 dollars to pay for what it was."

Back during the 1920's, compared to much higher prices today, Sister Warner remembered, "A pack of chewing gum was 5 cents. A stick of gum was 1 cent. Little drops of candy were 1 cent too. Good shoes were only $2.98. Now, you pay $100 dollars for them, and they're no better than any pair of shoes because they're all made alike. So, you get the same shoe today for all that money, and back then, if you bought a $5 pair of shoes, you were rich. Some of the stores back then were: Kanes, Landsburgh, Jellef, Woodies (Woodward & Lothrop), Palace Royal, and Hechts (all White stores). The only stores for Colored people in Washington, DC, were on 7th Street and Rhode Island Avenue downtown, and they were Harry Kaufmann and Goldenburgs." Sister

Warner stated that these stores were owned by Jewish people, but they were patronized by African Americans.

According to her rich recollection of times gone by, "We didn't have credit cards back then. If you saw something in the window and liked it, you'd go in there and pay $2, and you could take it home, and they'll come every Monday morning to where you lived and get the $2. You could go back to the store and pay them once a week, but if you didn't go to the store to pay on your bill weekly, they (people from the store) would come to your house to get their money. Yes, they were like bill collectors."

Remembering a costly lesson, Sister Warner said, "The thing that taught me a lesson once was I needed a coat, and my two sisters needed coats also. I went to Harry Kaufmann down on 7th Street, and I got 3 coats, and the 3 coats cost about $150. That was the hardest thing in the world to pay for. That was a lot of money, $150. That was one thing that taught me a lesson. I'll never buy anything if I can't pay for it (on the spot with money). I'll leave it in the store because money was short, and my father was out of work."

She continued, "He (my father) had worked in the mines, and the coal miners had gone on strike, and sometimes you got money, and sometimes you didn't. I couldn't take the coats back. So I struggled. I paid for them. They would come to our house for $2 week after week, and that taught me a lesson. I don't buy anything that I can not pay for. People get into trouble with those charge cards. I have one, but I don't use it much, just very, very seldom. I use it, but I don't get anymore than I can pay for by the month. If I can't pay for it during that month, then it stays in the store."

Tonsa's remembrances of racism were spoken about and are as follows: "You couldn't even go to Georgetown and buy anything. That was 'lily white.' It was Colored first. Then, the White people took it over, and you had to be somebody to live in Georgetown. You couldn't afford what they had over there, no. Seventh Street was where the Colored people went. If you went downtown and tried on something, it was yours whether it fit or didn't. You didn't carry it back. You had to pay for it!"

According to Sister Warner, "Some of the people still have racist attitudes today. Some of the Colored people feel like if they have 2 or 3 dollars more than you do, they're better than you. Yes, they think if you have $5 and they have $10, they're a little better than you. The Colored people didn't try to help each other back then. If you were hungry, you'd just beg on the street, just didn't have anything. I like to help people. I have never been really hungry in my whole life because I always had food to eat. So, if a person says they are hungry, I don't know if they are hungry or not, but you give them something to eat. If it's a dollar or whatever you can give them, give it to them."

In the words of Tonsa Warner, "When I go into the church on Sabbath, the men, women, and little children come and give me a hug, don't say a word, just give me a hug, and it shows that there's love in it (love in the church). I guess age has a lot to do with it. When I first come in, they (deacons, ushers, or members) meet me and hug me and kiss me, and take me by the arm and take me in."

"That's like a little child who had drawn a picture for me. She came up to me, never said a word, and just gave it to me. They do that you know and come and speak and give me a hug and just keep going." What a blessing and privilege to share Tonsa's story with you, dear readers!

Now, it's a good thing to give, but isn't it just as good to receive every now and then?

Looking Back
by Nancy A. Link, Ph.D. ©2013

Looking back to days and years long gone,
Sister Warner's faith always kept her strong.
Looking back & remembering many things,
Sister Warner's faith, through it all, rings.
Looking back and thanking God for it all,
Sister Warner's faith in God still stands tall.

Sister Warner's son, the late McClain Larcello Lavett, also marched on Washington with Dr. Martin Luther King, Jr., and thousands of others in 1963, an historical moment he spoke about with respect, pride, and high esteem.

There are other facets of Sister Warner's life that I would be remiss to not discuss, i.e., her hat making and sewing abilities, and her scrumptious 'sweet potato ice cream.' First, let's delve into her awesome abilities as a hat maker and her outstanding performance as a seamstress. The following description tells us how to make a hat in Tonsa's own words.

Steps in making a hat

1. Block them – by getting a flat piece of paper, see you'd have to have all these blocks, that's why we went downtown (New York) to the bowers and you can get any kind of hat you wanted. They would block it out for you, and then you'd trim it up.

2. Long process – blocking involves getting really stiff hat material and the straw, they can sew it for you. You show them how you want it done and all of that. There's regular hat material that you can use. It's a long process if you get into it really big. It's brain work.

3. Have it framed, which is a stiff material (frame), and you have it blocked out the way you want it.

4. You put it on a hot machine and put glue on it the way you want it. Then you trim it the way you want it.

5. Cover it with silk, straw, leather, fur or whatever material preferred.

6. Of course, with cloth and fur, you just take the material and work with it like that.

7. Whatever design you want in there, you just work it in there.

8. You can sew them by going through the looped holes in a crocheting fashion.

How long it takes to make a hat depends on the materials you use in the hat-making process as well as the colors and other things you add to the hat. You can do it in one day if you put your mind to it. Tonsa added, "It (hat making) is tedious work and it's brain work, but I used to have hat shows, and it was enjoyable. This was in the 1930's to the 1960's."

In the words of this hat making expert, "I always wanted to make hats. It came to my mind that I wanted to make hats, and the first hat I made, I made it with silk. I just sat down one day, and this lady had a hat from the store, and I said, 'Let me try it.' And I made the hat, the first hat I made, and the woman bought it. I didn't make hats just for sale. I would take orders. I didn't have a shop. So, I would just take orders. Anybody that saw me with a hat would say, 'Would you make me a hat?' I made the deaconesses hats in the big church in New York. I think it was about 25 (hats that I made). It didn't take long to do it."

As a sensational seamstress, Sister Warner further commented, "I make my own clothes too, just about everything I wear, coats, suits, everything. I have a sewing machine here (at my home). I used to sew downstairs, but climbing up and down those stairs got to be too much. I used to make my coats and everything, get the material and make them just like they came out of the store. A coat, to me, is easier than a dress. You don't have the detail work in it like you do with a dress. People used to want me to sew for them, and I said, 'No, I just sew for myself.'"

Memories were recalled, "My mother never taught us to sew. She sewed, but she didn't sit down and say, 'Now this is the way you do this here.' We would watch her, and all of my sisters could sew. We would watch her (my mother). The first thing I made was an apron for my mother. I said, 'Mama, let me make you an apron.' My legs were too short. They had these peddle machines. You know you had to peddle it with your feet. So my brother, Henry Jester, he'd sit there, he was younger and next to me (in age), and he would run the machine, and I would hold the material, and I made my mother an apron, and she just carried on so much about how beautiful it was, and I just thought I was really a seamstress. I made my coats and everything. Well, you learn when you're poor. You learn how to do more things than one if you wanted to."

Sister Tonsa Warner decided that she would also share her 'Sweet Potato Ice Cream' recipe with us. She used to make this delicious treat for her grandchildren, especially during her days at Pine Forge. Try it. You might just like it. No, you will certainly love it!

Steps in Making Sweet Potato Ice Cream (Serving 8 to 10)

You would make it just like you would make any other kind of ice cream.

1. Take a generous amount of sweet potatoes and boil them.

2. After boiling, let them cool.

3. Then peel them, and mash them up with a sieve.

   (Run peeled potatoes through a sieve to remove stringy substance and have fine, smooth potatoes)

4. Add dairy cream (2 cups). The more cream, the richer and better the ice cream.

5. Add sugar (1 cup) or sweeten to your taste.

6. Add vanilla flavoring or whatever flavor you want (2 tablespoons).

7. Stir all ingredients together well (for several minutes) in an old fashioned ice cream churn.

8. Pour the freshly made ice cream in a bowl and freeze it, like you would do any other ice cream. Let it chill in the freezer, and it's delightful.

Note: Just like you buy peach ice cream or banana ice cream, it's like that. You would do it the same way.

You need an old fashioned ice cream churn (metal container and ice or rock salt is placed around the outside/edges). We had a big one (ice cream churn) at home when we were growing up. We had a 2 gallon freezer, and we would make ice cream on Sundays and things like that. We had the cream and everything to go into it. I still have my freezer. I haven't used it for so long.

As Sister Tonsa Warner's story of faith comes to its concluding pages, one must remember that "Nobody could tell you to be faithful. It has to come through you." These were words of wisdom shared by Sister Warner. Her journey of faith will be on-going, and so, I asked more questions, and she gave more answers. Therefore, dear reader, I have scripted the following questions and answers for you to ponder for yourself?

What advice would you give to others, especially young women, about faith in God and decision making?

"Well, you have to have a feeling inside yourself that you don't want to be a street walker. You want to do something that would make people feel proud of you, and you could be an example to other people just by looking at you. Like these girls out here today, they go out half-naked. Their clothes are up here almost at the top of their thighs, and they sit down, and they don't have anything to cover their nakedness. You don't go out like that. That's what I'm always preaching to them. Put some clothes on. You're tempting the men when you go out here half-naked. You put some clothes on so you'll be covered so when you sit down, you will have something over your knees. So, they come to church like that, and nobody will say anything."

To the young women, Sister Warner would also say, "You got to believe God. He made you. He knows what you're like. He made you, and He knows what He is doing. If you have a mind to pray and ask Him for something, don't fight it. Go with it, yes indeed. Just like when I sold my car, I didn't want to let it go, but He said to let it go. So, I just gave it up and didn't worry about it."

To the young men, Sister Warner would say, "Don't make a fool out of yourselves over the women. I mean life was so different when I came up. I was 16 years old when I left home, and men didn't excite me. I was never raised that way that you just had to have somebody hanging on to you, and I think what has ruined these young girls and young boys today is cars. They get in these cars and go out, and that's the end of their life like that, and the girl comes back, and she got a baby, and he's gone on giving somebody else another one, and that's the way it goes."

Moreover, she expressed, "And they get out here, and they think they're not a man until they get a cigarette in their mouth or a glass in their hand with liquor in it. They can't be a man until they do that??? Their heads are not working right. I tell you the truth. I think the courts have really ruined the young people because now you can't correct your child. If you correct (spank) that child, you go to jail. All he's got to do is get on the telephone and call the police – say, 'child abuse,' and here they (the police) come, and you (parents) got to pay for it. Your own child, you can't correct them, and so they know that. So they're going to defy their parents and do what they want to do because they know they have protection."

Regarding faith and decision making, what would you say to the young men who are trying to serve God?

"Well, I would praise them. I would tell them how nice they are being and all of that. Just like a lot of young people at Pine Forge, when I was there, they were talking about marrying and having babies. Well, it's a time for all of that. You don't rush it. It's a time for it. Well, this girl (at Pine Forge Academy in Pottstown, Pennsylvania), she was going with (dating) this boy, and he was at Oakwood College (in Huntsville, Alabama), and he came to visit her, and that was his last year at Oakwood, and he didn't want to marry yet because he didn't have anything. He was just trying to finish school, and she decided, oh, she didn't want to wait. She wanted to get married. So, she went out and met this other guy, and he was as mean to her as a snake, and finally, she had to leave him. So, I guess you just have to listen sometimes when people try to help you."

How do you think people think someone 100 years of age should look?

"People think a 100 year old person should be decrepit and drawn up. For example, I was on the train one time coming from Florida, and this White guy sat beside me and was running his mouth and was questioning me about some things, and I said, 'I think I'm a little older than you are. I'm 90 years old.' He looked at me and jumped up and said, 'This woman is 90 years old. Where are the wrinkles?' Everybody was pointing. I said, 'Now mercy!'"

During the Summer of 2002 (June), Sister Warner and her youngest sister Taqua were changing trains on their way to New Mexico. Sister Warner told the story as follows. "Another story I remember is of this White woman who was standing up with a little boy, and she said, 'Somebody had said you were 100 years old.' So, she said she started to come over and take my picture, but she didn't want to come over without asking. So she finally said, 'Could I take your picture? I heard you were 100 years old.' I said, 'Certainly.' So, the little boy wanted to come over and hug me, and he gave me a big hug because he never hugged a 100 year old lady." As Sister Warner's story continues developing in the final chapter of her story of faith, Chapter 11, sit back, relax, and read on dear reader, some memorable 'quotations and poetic salutations.'

Sister Tonsa Warner celebrating 100 years of faithful living

```
************************************
```

CHAPTER ELEVEN

```
************************************
```

"Who is wise and understanding among you? Let him show it by his good life, by deed done in the humility that comes from wisdom" (James 3:13, NIV).

Quotations and Poetic Salutations

From the wilderness of West Virginia to the wonders of Washington, DC, Tonsa Nella Fuqua Lavett Warner bravely survived 103 years as a living testimony to God's goodness and faithfulness to her. Like people throughout history, her story is one of togetherness, courage, strength, faith, determination, love, joy, excitement, and so much more. As her journey of faith in God continues to develop to the point of culmination, there were many memories and thoughts that were recalled during our interview sessions. Therefore, after analyzing and interpreting the collected data from Sister Warner, her story continues with quotations from Tonsa Warner augmented by poetic salutations from the writer's electronic pen.

Quotations from Tonsa Warner

"It's nothing too hard for God, nothing."

"We have made mistakes, so we can go to Him, and He'll forgive us if we go to Him in faith and believe and turn from it."

"You don't have anything to give each other but kind words."

"The hardest thing to do is to turn your family around."

"As a Christian, I just feel God has blessed me, and whatever I go to do, I pray over it."

"Wherever I go out the door, I just ask God to take me."

"I always put God first in everything."

"As for people, everybody's just people to me."

"God is the Great Creator and Wonderful Person."

"God watches over us."

"Everything good that comes to you comes from God the Father, God the Son, and God the Holy Spirit."

"You don't speak harsh to people."

"If you don't have a kind word to say to a person, don't say anything at all."

"A smile will just get you a long way sometimes."

"There is no boss in marriage."

"Faith and patience work together."

"It only takes a little faith for prayers to be answered."

"Don't ever think you're better than anybody else."

"It's only the grace of God that keeps us."

"You learn from everybody, even a child."

"You can learn something from anyone."

"As long as you take care of your responsibilities, you can go wherever you want to go."

"I'm a person who loves to go."

"The Sabbath is about being faithful, fearing God (loving and respecting Him), and keeping His commandments."

"You have to believe God is going to hear you before you ask Him."

"Pictures let you watch your change in life."

"I believe in God and call on Him when I need Him."

"You should live each day with His watch care and guidance."

"God gives you what you need."

"You can't love and hate."

"Every answer you need is right there in the Bible."

"God answers prayers the way that's best for you."

"Avoid jealousy; be thankful for God's blessings."

In the following poetic salutations, I (as the author of this book) earnestly consider it an honor and privilege to be able to salute Sister Tonsa Warner with the art of poetry. Since my early school days, I have viewed writing as exciting. Therefore, I conclude this story with poems that express many facets of this story of faith, a story on the life and times of Sister Tonsa Warner. I would like to thank you Sister Warner for sharing your story. In addition, thank you dear reader(s) for going on this journey of faith with Sister Tonsa Warner and me. May God continue to bless us all through it all!

Poetic Salutations
"If I could . . . ."
By Nancy A. Link, Ph.D.

If I could live my life all over again,

I wouldn't change too much, no ma'am.

If I could live my life all over again,

I'd treat people right for I am who I am.

If I could live my life all over again,

I'd be just as happy as I am right now.

If I could live my life all over again,

I'd praise God, yes, praise Him anyhow.

If I could live my life all over again,

I'd humbly serve just like I always enjoyed,

If I could live my life all over again,

I'd just keep on trusting & obeying the Lord.

If I could live my life all over again,

I'd embrace faith, hope, and love always,

If I could live my life all over again,

I'd constantly thank God all of my days.

My Father Was a Hard Worker

By Nancy A. Link, Ph.D.

My father was a hard worker & made ends meet,
He made sure we always had some food to eat.
My father worked in the coal mines of West Virginia,
Then, one day, he bought us a big farm in Virginia.

My father was a hard worker, and I love him for that,
I'll never forget that little light on his coal mining hat.
My father was a great man and strictly business, I'd say,
He showed us love and lots of joy on a sunny or rainy day.

My father was a hard worker because he was a good man,
He did what he could to provide and help us understand.
My father wanted us to understand the value of a dollar,
I thank God for my father, who would never even holler.

Tonsa's parents: Mr. Henry June Fuqua (sitting) and his wife, Mrs.
Nellie Otey Fuqua (standing), 1925

Obeying My Mother

By Nancy A. Link, Ph.D.

Obeying my mother was such a joy for me,
It made me feel so very wonderful, you see.
My mother was a Christian and teacher too,
She taught us at home the things to say & do.

Obeying my mother was a blessing for me,
For I've lived over 100 years, wonderfully free.
My mother was a woman, who believed in God,
I remember so well, "For God, nothing's too hard."

Obeying my mother is something I still do, oh yes,
I know she taught me right because I feel blessed.
If my mother was here today, it would be "yes ma'am,"
I thank you for training me well to obey The Great I Am.

Tonsa Fuqua Lavett Warner's mother,
Mrs. Nellie Ann Otey Fuqua, 1941

My Brothers and Sisters
By Nancy A. Link, Ph.D.

My brothers and sisters really made life worthwhile,
I will always remember the way they made me smile.
We worked and played together on a Virginian farm,
We looked out for one another & nobody did us harm.

My brothers and sisters were always there for me,
Even o'er the miles & years, we communicated, you see.
Through the happiness and joy, the grief and the pain,
We believed in togetherness, again and again and again.

My brothers and sisters? Most of them are gone on now,
Yet, they remain in my heart, and memories linger anyhow.
I thank God for my mind, and for my heart, and for my soul,
I'll always thank God for family and for good times untold.

Photos from the 1920's

Tonsa's eldest sister,
Lucinda Fuqua
Gravett

Tonsa and her
brother, Rossie Otey
Fuqua

Tonsa and her sister,
Calestard Fuqua

Tonsa (Right) and a
family friend

Tonsa (front seat)
and her sister,
Calestard (back
seat), in Rolls Royce

(L to R) Taqua,
Tonsa, Friend, and
Lucinda

Just the Three of Us

By Nancy A. Link, Ph.D.

Just the three of us together again after all these years,
Thinking of the early days in DC mingled with the tears.
The Lord in His great mercy has brought us three through,
From then until now, God Almighty knew just what to do.

Just the three of us together again, I am so full of joy,
Thinking back to being separated, like a broken toy.
I remember my children, my little boy and my little girl,
I'm so happy to be with you now, in this, my Father's world.

Just the three of us together again in our great latter days,
Thinking about the changes, and about how praying pays.
It's a blessing for Sister Warner & her children, Bunny & Sis,
To be together in any kind of weather, oh what awesome bliss!

"THE THREE OF US TOGETHER AGAIN
AFTER ALL THOSE YEARS"
In Photo: Violet Barnhart "Sis" (Left), McClain Larcello Lavett "Bunny"
(Middle), and Sister Tonsa Warner (Right), 2002

Yahweh is Da Way

By Nancy A. Link, PhD ©2003

Yahweh is da way and my forever Friend,
He is God Almighty from beginning to end.
Yahweh is da way, and that is for certain,
He's omniscient & knows when were hurtin'.

Yahweh is da way, oh for sure dear brother,
He is God, and beside Him, there's no other.
Yahweh is da way, it's really true my sister,
He's Lord of Lords and King of Kings Mister.

Yahweh is da way throughout this mortal life,
He is our God through the struggles & strife.
Yahweh is da way throughout the all and all,
He sustains us Winter, Spring, Summer & Fall.

Yahweh is da way, over & over & over, oh yes,
He is Jehovah-jireh, and He's forever the Best.
Yahweh is da way, He's Father, our great God,
He's Almighty, and for God, nothing's too hard.

Yahweh is da way to eternal life & immortality,
He is the great "I am" and helps us with reality.
Yahweh is da way; daily blessings we receive,
God's Word is truth; just trust, obey & believe!

In Summary

As the interviews came to a close, I knew this was a story that had to be told. So, you have it, *Over 100 Years of Faith in God, The Story of Sister Tonsa Warner.* Consequently, in our final formal interview session, the question was asked, "Sister Warner, is there anything in your life you would have done differently?" Her response was simply, yet eloquently articulated, "I don't think there was anything I would have done differently. I tried to live a clean life, a good life, helping others and doing what I could, and that was it."

One last question that I would have been remiss to not ask was, "What would you say to others to encourage them or give them advice when it comes to living long, healthy, Godly lives?" The answer, as it flowed from the narrative voice of Sister Tonsa Warner, was, "You just try to live right, and treat everybody the same or the way you want to be treated yourself. You don't say harsh words to them. Be kind to them and all of that. If you see somebody doing something they shouldn't be doing, you don't jump on them with both feet. You try to talk to them and tell them how wrong they are and show them the right way. Love will carry you farther than hate."